Wisconsin Folklife

A Celebration of Wisconsin Traditions

Cover photos, from top:

Norm Dombrowski and the Happy Notes strike a pose before they strike up a polka. Photo courtesy of Norm Dombrowski.

Dang Yang of Milwaukee displays the *qeej*, a traditional Hmong instrument. Photo by Mai Zong Vue.

Packer fans love tailgating at Lambeau Field, Green Bay. Photo by Andy Kraushaar.

Preparation begins for the Nativity Blessed Virgin Mary parish *booyah* and smelt dinner in Tisch Mills. Photo by Andy Kraushaar.

LeRoy R. Lee, Publisher
Marshall Cook, Editor
Lynn Hanus, Managing Editor
Barry Carlsen, University Publications, Designer
Eileen Fitzgerald, University Publications, Production Editor
Printed by Times Printing

Table of Contents

TOMMY G. THOMPSON

Governor
State of Wisconsin

Greetings!

Our yearlong Sesquicentennial celebration offers a great opportunity to explore Wisconsin's unique heritage, to revisit old friends, and to make new ones.

The variety of sights, sounds, and tastes that makes us Wisconsin, America's shining star, is truly amazing. Wisconsin's ethnic potpourri, colorful traditions, quality craftsmanship, and love of the outdoors have made us a state unlike any other.

People who visited us at the Smithsonian Folklife Festival 1998 in Washington, D.C., said Wisconsin people seem to have a special appreciation for life. As the Wisconsin Folklife Festival comes home to Wisconsin's Capitol Square, bigger and even better, the celebration continues, with hundreds of festival participants sharing the vitality and delightful abundance of "America's State."

The publication you are holding is a folklife festival in print. It captures the rich tapestry of life in Wisconsin: from fishing to high-tech dairying, from the Ojibwe through the recently arrived Hmong, from handmade crafts to brand-name products instantly known around the world, from the polka to the Packers.

Wisconsin Folklife: A Celebration of Wisconsin Traditions will be a keepsake of the Wisconsin Sesquicentennial you will want to share with your family for generations to come.

Sincerely,

Tommy G. Thompson
Governor

Room 115 East, State Capitol, P.O. Box 7863, Madison, Wisconsin 53707 • (608)266-1212 • FAX (608)267-8983

Wisconsin Folklife

Wisconsin lies in the heart of a distinctive region of America, the Upper Midwest. A unique way of life has developed here, a regional culture shaped by its varied people and striking natural environment. Moreover, the European immigrants who settled in Wisconsin during the nineteenth century brought concepts of civic participation and land stewardship that have deeply influenced social, cultural, economic, and ecological activity in the state, making an impact on the state's folklife.

In Wisconsin an attachment to the community and its roots remains significant in everyday life. Volunteers run community fish fries, dairy breakfasts, church lutefisk dinners or *booyah* picnics; organize parades for *Syttende Mai* (Norwegian Constitution Day), Cheese Days, and Polish Constitution Day; and teach their kids to dance a *laendler, kolo, tarantella,* or *schottische,* or to play a *qeej,* accordion, *tamburitza,* or *shekeree.*

Wisconsinites engage the state's lands and waters, experiencing the extremes of the seasons and using and conserving natural resources. Normal life is suspended during deer season each November when 800,000 hunters head for the woods. Fishing is pervasive in every season and, because so many people enjoy the sport, live bait dispensers are located in many filling stations. Fishers in waders lure brook trout to hand-tied flies. On thousands of Wisconsin lakes, bluegills and crappies are hooked from shore, piers, and boats, or pulled up through the thick winter ice into fishing shanties.

In the spring, mushroom pickers harvest morels from jealously guarded secret spots. Canoes are stacked on many Wisconsin porches and beside garages ready to hit the water.

As fall slides into winter, football fans socialize in stadium parking lots over bratwurst and beer at tailgate parties that start at dawn and don't end until after dusk. Kids figure skate or play pick-up hockey games at the park lagoon.

Much of the southern two-thirds of Wisconsin's rolling landscape is dominated by family dairy farms. During the mid-nineteenth century, dairy farmers from upstate New York and central Europe established an enduring agricultural practice suited to Wisconsin's land and climate. Dairy farmers typically provide much of their own hay and corn. These fodder crops nourish the dairy herds that have been bred to produce large quantities of milk. The cattle generate other by-products, such as meat, leather, and fertilizer. Nowadays even the whey is processed into valuable lactose and protein products.

A large majority of the milk produced in Wisconsin is processed into 250 varieties of cheese in the many cheese factories in small and large towns throughout the state. Wisconsin produces 30 percent of the cheese in the United States, using cheese-making skills and practices evolved from Old World traditions.

The land use pattern associated with dairy farming contributes to the striking beauty of Wisconsin's landscape. Corn and alfalfa fields surround neat farmsteads dominated by huge barns and towering silos. Dairy farmers preserve woodlands on their farms to meet timber needs and to provide habitat for the deer harvested in fall for venison.

Family dairy farms contribute to community stability and the persistence of traditions. In hundreds of Wisconsin communities, the family names in the current telephone directory match those on the headstones in the cemetery. Descendants of nineteenth-century settlers make up much of the populace in Wisconsin towns, often lending them an ethnic identity. Westby is Norwegian, Pilsen is Czech, Rosiere is Belgian, Mayville is German, Monroe is Swiss, and Little Chute is Dutch.

An active citizenry governs Wisconsin towns and cities with ideas stemming from the mid-nineteenth century anti-monarchist revolutions in central Europe. Idealistic leaders, especially from the ranks of the so-called German "Forty-eighters," sought to establish a just and participatory society in their new homeland. Examples of their legacy are still found in local control of infrastructure, in active rural township government, and in a history of pioneering efforts toward industrial democracy.

These stable and participatory communities have spawned Wisconsin folklife, and the varied traditions have influenced one another. The Belgians of southern Door County have embraced the brass band dance music of their Czech neighbors in Kewaunee County, for example, while the Czech Catholic parish picnics in the area serve up the Belgians' *booyah* soup from sixty gallon cauldrons.

People of northern and central European origins have been the most numerous, but immigrants from all over the world spice the Wisconsin cultural mix. In this ethnic stew, some Old World folkways like the making of Norwegian Hardanger fiddles or the weaving of Latvian sashes have been preserved or revived similar to their original form. Other traditions like polka music and dancing or quilting are truly American, having developed from a mixture, a kind of "creolization" of the contributions of various cultural groups living side by side in Wisconsin.

The climate, geography, and economy of Wisconsin have shaped many shared regional traditions. The abundant timber of Wisconsin's forests provides the basis for timber harvesting folklife and prompts vital woodworking traditions. Wisconsin's inland "seashores" on Lakes Superior and Michigan and the thousands of lakes dotting Wisconsin's glacial landscape have stimulated boat building and fishing traditions. The central North American climate, with its hot summers and cold winters, has produced an annual cycle of activities suited to the seasons. Wisconsinites tap maple trees and dip smelt in the spring, cut hay, pick cherries, or welcome tourists to lakeside resorts in summer, and harvest corn and cranberries and hunt geese in the fall.

Community festivals crowd Wisconsin's warmer months, but Wisconsinites' famed propensity for partying also defies the cold. Wisconsinites celebrate winter carnivals, compete in ski races and ice fishing tournaments, and turn the parking lot of Lambeau Field into a cold weather Mardi Gras for every Green Bay Packers home game.

Cultural sharing began with what the Europeans learned from Native Americans. European immigrants observed the fishing, hunting, and gathering practices of the Woodland Indian tribes. Native practices influenced the way European immigrants began to tap maple trees for sugar, gather and use wild rice, fish for walleyes and muskellunge, and hunt deer. For example, nineteenth-century German American farmers in the Lake Winnebago area observed indigenous Ho-Chunk fishers spearing sturgeons through the February ice and took up the practice themselves. Today the descendants of those immigrants assemble a temporary village of some four to five thousand ice fishing shanties on Lake Winnebago. Inside the shanties, with spears at the ready, these fishers peer into the greenish water, some listening to polkas on AM radio from nearby Chilton, others sipping homemade honey wine made from Wisconsin wild grapes and an Old World recipe, all hoping and waiting for the rare moment when a monstrous five- to eight-foot sturgeon might come nosing around their submerged fish decoy.

At the end of the nineteenth and through the twentieth century, arrivals of southern and eastern Europeans, African

Americans, Asians, and Latinos have enriched the cultural landscape. The most numerous eastern Europeans are Polish Americans, with substantial communities in Wisconsin industrial towns. Milwaukee's south side, with Polish ethnic landmarks like the St. Josephat Basilica and the shrine to St. Mary Czestohowa at St. Stanislaus Church, is the state's largest "Polonia" (the nickname for a compact Polish American neighborhood). Restaurants offer traditional Polish foods like *pierogi* and *czarnina*. Numerous Polish lodges, social clubs, soccer teams, choirs, and folk dance groups pursue Polish religious and social customs. Artisans like Bernice Jendrzejczak, a maker of *wycinanki* (paper cut art), practice Polish handicrafts.

Milwaukee's large African American community boasts a strong tradition of gospel music and traditional crafts like quilting and doll making. The Queens of Harmony sing traditional a cappella gospel. Velma Seales and Blanche Shankle are active in a Milwaukee women's quilt group. George McCormick carves and dresses wooden dolls, while Mary Leazer's making of traditional rag dolls has drawn her husband, George Leazer, into the creation of dioramas comprised of his handmade clay dolls arranged to depict African American social customs.

While earlier immigrants came to farm, cut timber, or mine ores, the industrial cities of southeastern Wisconsin increasingly attracted new arrivals to work in factories, mills, foundries, and packing houses, on the docks and shipyards of Great Lakes ports, and in railway shops and roundhouses. Today southeastern Wisconsin abounds with skilled machinists who create construction equipment, farm implements, and tools. A few, like retired millwright Roy Treder, have turned these skills to artistic pursuits. When a retirement gift is needed for a fellow worker at Milwaukee's Harley-Davidson motorcycle factory, Roy welds an elaborate base for a clock or lamp from tools and machinery parts symbolic of that fellow worker's career. Roy has created more than 200 such retirement gift sculptures.

Wisconsin's industrial towns and cities are a patchwork of urban ethnic villages, neighborhoods comprised of blocks of well-kept modest frame houses with churches and taverns on the street corners. The church basement and the corner bar have served these neighborhoods as welcoming social centers, much as do the churches and crossroads taverns in Wisconsin's rural areas. In both urban and rural communities, traditional music, dance, crafts, foodways, and religious traditions have been preserved through generations in these twin hubs of community social life.

Many religious communities have an ethnic as well as a denominational aspect. One Lutheran church might attract primarily Norwegian parishioners, while another appeals to Germans. Catholic churches may be predominantly Polish, German, Irish, Mexican, Italian, Croatian, or Slovak. Services may be offered in the language of the old homeland as well as in English. Church women's clubs and altar societies practice ethnic crafts and foodways.

Taverns provide another venue for ethnic or regional traditions. Polka dancers twirl to the concertina player's tunes at a wedding in the church hall or at the local Friday night fish fry in a tavern down the road. Elfrieda Haese remembers the women of her community catching up on gossip while knitting in a booth in Schaegler's Tavern in Milwaukee while the men played cards or sang.

Friday night in Wisconsin means taking the whole family to a tavern for a fish fry. Taverns participate in softball and bowling leagues, organize group outings to sports events, and host card games like euchre, cribbage, and sheepshead, and indoor sports like darts and duck pins, a scaled-down bowling game.

The crossroads bar may serve as a Wisconsin Department of Natural Resources registration station during hunting and fishing seasons. Snapshots of hunters and fishers weighing or measuring their catches may be taped to the walls. Some taverns serve as local museums with historic photographs, old-fashioned farming or logging tools, or record-sized muskies or sturgeon or bucks' heads displayed on the walls. Musical instruments, for display or play, adorn many taverns.

Whether expressed through church, tavern, or home, the role of ethnic identity remains prominent in Wisconsin. Fourth and fifth generation Americans are still aware of their ethnic origins. When folks meet here, they may ask after the ethnic provenance of their last names. Recent immigrants speak Spanish, Laotian, or Hmong. Families whose forebears immigrated generations ago still speak German, Polish, Norwegian, or the Walloon dialect of French in their homes. Children learn ethnic identity in folk dance groups and ethnic orchestras, an important reason why ethnicity remains so pervasive in the state.

Traditional arts mark ethnic identity. Norwegian Americans emphasize rosemaling, acanthus carving, and Hardanger lace making. Among the Slavic nationalities in Wisconsin, Ukrainians stress *pysanki* Easter eggs and cross-stitch embroidery, and Slovaks have wheat weavings. Other Slavs use a musical instrument in a symbolic role; Serbians have the one-stringed *gusle*, Slovenians the diatonic button accordion, and Croatians the lute-like *tamburitza*.

Many ethnic groups create crafts primarily for display in the home to indicate heritage. Crafts also retain their pragmatic purposes. Mary Lou Schneider and Willi Kruschinski seek to design the perfect lure to catch game fish. Members of the Lac du Flambeau band of Ojibwe create ice fishing decoys in the shape of minnows to use and display. Today decoy carvers like Brooks Big John make some purely decorative decoys, attached perhaps to pieces of driftwood or to lamp bases, a decorative symbol of Lac du Flambeau heritage. But Brooks also carves decoys that are carefully weighted and fitted with tin fins so they will "swim" realistically in the water when he is ice fishing, so he can land a big fish for his family's dinner table.

New immigration continues to enrich Wisconsin folklife. Refugees from wars and political oppression find a haven in the state. Wisconsin now has America's second largest population of Hmong, Southeast Asian refugees who actively pursue their unique music, crafts, and social customs in the new homeland. Wisconsin also has one of the major settlements of Tibetans. Lama Ngawang Chojor, a Tibetan Buddhist monk living in Madison, is adept at making elaborate sand mandala paintings.

Latino populations in the state have increased markedly in recent decades, the largest being of Mexican origin. Many Wisconsin Mexican Americans are the descendants of seasonal agricultural workers who came from the Southwest and northern Mexico to work in Wisconsin fields, frozen food plants, and canneries. Today they preserve music, crafts, and foodways in their urban community in Milwaukee and in a number of smaller agricultural towns. The second largest Latino group, Puerto Ricans, live mainly in Milwaukee, where Miguel Cruz makes the traditional musical instrument of Puerto Rican *jibaro* villagers, the *cuatro*.

The Wisconsin program at the Smithsonian Folklife Festival in Washington, D.C., and its restaging in Madison as the Wisconsin Folklife Festival in August of 1998 honor the many people who preserve Wisconsin's folklife and mark Wisconsin's Sesquicentennial of statehood. The program participants are outstanding bearers of significant traditions, and all offer evidence of the natural, cultural, and historical forces that have molded Wisconsin's unique and vital folklife. 🐦

Richard March
May 1998

The Enduring Craftsmanship of Wisconsin's Native Peoples: The Ojibwe Birchbark Canoe

by Thomas Vennum, Jr.

"The bark canoe of the Chippeways (Ojibwe) is, perhaps, the most beautiful and light model of all the water crafts that were ever invented. They are generally made complete with the rind of one birch tree, and so ingeniously shaped and sewed together, with roots of the tamarack . . . that they are water-tight and ride upon the water, as light as a cork. They gracefully lean and dodge about, under the skilful balance of an Indian . . but like everything wild, are timid and treacherous under the guidance of [a] white man; and, if he be not an equilibrist, he is sure to get two or three times soused, in his first endeavors at familiar acquaintance with them."

George Catlin, *Letters and Notes of the Manners, Customs and Condition of the North American Indian* (London, 1841).

Centuries-old Wisconsin Indian traditions continue to flourish and develop, not only in the decorative arts but also in the manufacture of utilitarian objects.

For example, Wisconsin Menominee, Potawatomi, and Ojibwe still produce bark containers traditionally used to store wild rice and maple sugar, historically the principal subsistence foods of woodlands Indians in the western Great Lakes area. As metal and plastic became available, Indian people adapted them to age-old technologies.

Perhaps no item in the traditional economy combines finesse and craftsmanship better than the birchbark canoe, historically the principal mode of transportation and cargo-freighting for Indian peoples in the western woodlands. Early travelers in the American wilderness were amazed by this unfamiliar type of boat and rarely failed to comment on its construction. Most scholars agree with the nineteenth-century artist George Catlin that the Ojibwe more than any other people brought canoe building to a fine art.

Although the birchbark canoe today has been supplanted by wooden, metal, and plastic boats, a handful of Ojibwe craftsmen

Photo by Janet Cardie

Earl Nyholm and Charlie Ashmun tie canoe inner and outer form stakes together; stones are used to weigh down and stabilize the canoe form.

The fourteen-foot canoe is ready to be launched.

retain the knowledge of every step in its traditional manufacture and the skills needed to apply them.

In the summer of 1997, a film crew from the Smithsonian's folklife office documented the construction of a traditional Ojibwe canoe. A grant from the Wisconsin Sesquicentennial Commission funded the film. Earl Nyholm, a professor of the Ojibwe language at Bemidji State University in Minnesota, served as master builder. Earl's eighty-four-year-old mother, Julia, assisted, along with Mark Wabanikee, an apprentice from Bear Island in Lake Michigan, several of Earl's relatives living on the Bad River Reservation in Wisconsin, and a craftswoman from the Red Cliff Reservation, Diane Defoe.

The five weeks of construction took place on a Lake Superior beach on Madeline Island, the ancestral homeland of the Ojibwe people. The site was in fact the location of the first trading post of the Northwest Fur Company in the eighteenth century; undoubtedly this very beach had witnessed canoe construction in earlier times.

The process must always begin with the search for the proper birch tree. The German cartographer Johann Kohl visited Madeline Island in 1854 and noted the importance of good bark for the canoe in his 1860 book, *Kitchi-Gami, Wanderings round Lake Superior:* "The Indians expend as many bark canoes as we do hunting-boots. . . . The largest and smoothest trees are selected, so that the pieces of bark may be as large as possible, and prevent too much sewing."

Canoe builders have a trained eye for picking out a "canoe birchbark tree," which ideally should be some fifty to sixty inches in diameter. Due to the decimation of forests for lumber and pulpwood, birch trees this size are a rarity today. Furthermore, the tree must be straight and free of "eyes" and lichen growth that might cause the bark to tear under pressure. Also, the tree must not bifurcate at its top.

Earl suggested that only one in a hundred trees meets these qualifications.

Having rejected for imperfections a number of large trees identified in advance, his search ended after five days in a wilderness preserve on Madeline Island with the discovery of a fifty-four-inch tree.

Canoe builders need a single large piece to run the length of the bottom of the vessel. If the bark isn't wide enough to reach the gunwales on either side, it requires "piecing." That is, bark must be added along the gunwale at the widest part of the

"Most scholars agree with the nineteenth-century artist George Catlin that the Ojibwe more than any other people brought canoe building to a fine art."

canoe. Such "pieced" bark requires double-stitch sewing for its length, which is very time-consuming. Thus, the harvest of large birch by the dominant society hastened the decline of the craft of building bark canoes.

Some builders will fell the tree, but Earl likes to take his bark from a standing tree. The removal of bark does not kill the tree immediately, since the exposed cadmium layer will heal, but the tree will eventually die. Taking the bark at precisely the right time is essential, for there is only about a five-day period in late June with the right day and nighttime temperatures. Builders make two circumference incisions and join them with a straight vertical cut.

The bark of the birch Earl selected was clearly ripe for taking, as it virtually sprang off the tree with a loud zipping noise. Several days later it would have been virtually irremovable.

The builders then evenly spread a flat rectangular bed of sand and picked out rocks and twigs. They improvised a wigwam framework over this building area to accommodate tarps. These kept the canoe out of direct sunlight, preventing bark from drying too quickly and curling.

On the level bed of sand, Earl spread out the piece of bottom bark with its exterior (the white side) facing upward. (Miniature canoes made for sale to tourists

Photo by Richard March

Canoe building on Lake Superior's Madeline Island is a group effort.

mistakenly give the impression that the outside of the tree becomes the exterior of the canoe.) They placed an elliptical wooden canoe form with pointed ends on the bottom bark and weighted it down with rocks to stabilize it.

Ojibwe believe that their cultural hero, the legendary Wenabozho, invented the canoe for them. They will point to a pile of rocks on one of the Apostle Islands, saying these were the ones he used to weigh down the form of the first canoe.

Earl and his crew brought the bark up outside the length of the canoe and drove large birch canoe stakes into the ground along each side the length of the canoe to begin to form its shape. They clamped ends of the bottom piece together using "Indian clothes pins" made of cedar and tied the outer stakes to inner stakes with "Indian string," pieces of the inner bark of the basswood tree.

Because the bottom bark wasn't wide enough to reach from gunwale to gunwale at the canoe's midpoint, builders added a strip of bark to sew ("piece") on either side for a

Canoes Can Carry a Ton

The fourteen-foot canoe Earl built for the filming was fairly typical of a "family-size" two-person vessel. During the fur trade era much larger canoes were built for long-distance freighting on the Great Lakes. McKenney described a thirty-foot canoe that he estimated could carry 2,000 pounds. Kohl was amazed at how much Indians could pack into a canoe. He described a family from 150 miles into the interior of Wisconsin arriving on Madeline Island. As the father and one son glided the canoe into an inlet, he observed, "The wife, with her other children, two boys and two girls, was buried beneath a pile of parcels and boxes. Among them lay a dog, with three pups. And on top of all the plunder was a large cage, with two tamed falcons in it. The gunwale of the boat was only a few inches above the water, and in this way all these beings, and animals, and lumber, had made a seven day's voyage."

length of perhaps three feet. The women do all sewing, using roots of the jackpine tree split and kept in water until needed. Julia and Diane attended to this laborious task. Each stitch must be doubled for strength, that is, brought over and under each side of the overlapped bark. To accommodate the stitches, they used an awl to poke holes through the bark.

In his famous poem *Hiawatha*, Longfellow, basing his information on Henry Schoolcraft's Ojibwe research, extolled the creation of the canoe from natural resources:

> All the forest's life was in it,
> All its mystery and magic,
> All the lightness of a birch-tree,
> All the toughness of the cedar,
> All the larch's sinew supple.

Thomas McKenney, touring the area around Madeline Island in the mid-nineteenth century, praised the Indian talent for using only natural materials in canoe construction. "The Indians make no use of nails and screws," he wrote in his *Sketches of a Tour to the Lakes* in 1827. "[E]verything is sewn and tied together. But the seams, stitches, and knots are so regular, firm, and artistic, that nothing better could be asked for."

Next the builders created the long, thin cedar gunwales, both an outwale and inwale, the latter mortised to receive the tapered butt ends of three cedar thwarts to hold the top of the canoe apart. Once in place, the gunwales were lashed to each other and to the bark for the full perimeter of the vessel. At this point Earl, as master craftsman, fulfilled the custom of completing the finishing work at both ends by inserting an elaborately constructed cedar prow piece.

The next and crucial step in construction involved bending and inserting the cedar ribs, which gave the canoe its final rounded shape. About forty thin cedar ribs had been soaking for several

Photos by Janet Cardle

Photos from top: Detail of the gunwale assembly; canoe prow assembly with "man-board," made from a single piece of split cedar; interior view of the canoe with cedar planking in place.

days to make them more pliable. Still, the builders had to pour boiling water over them to increase their pliancy. Bending the ribs is a most frustrating time for every canoe builder. Despite all the soaking and heating, the ribs are still quite brittle and easily broken. Canoe builders always prepare additional ribs, knowing they can expect to break several in the bending process.

Wearing a special pair of moccasins, Earl stood on a pair of ribs and gradually pulled up on either end until he achieved the proper bend, then carried it to the canoe to insert it in place. Once all the ribs were intact, the canoe dried for a day, and then builders removed the ribs and inserted thin cedar planking, constituting "flooring," running the length of the craft. Builders then reinserted the ribs to hold the planking in place.

They installed a gunwale cap over the gunwale assembly with birchwood pegs.

The cap protects the lashing holding it together. They inverted the canoe for "pitching" to make watertight the places where the bark had been cut and sewn. They used pitch made from spruce gum and deer tallow, heated and melted down, with black charcoal from a maple log added for coloring. Ojibwe canoers always kept a small supply of pitch with them for repairs, just as a bicyclist carries a patch kit.

As soon as the pitch dried, the canoe was ready to launch. Wearing beautiful Ojibwe black velveteen vests adorned in typical curvilinear beadwork representing flowers and leaves, Earl and Julia climbed aboard and paddled off into the sunset to provide the Smithsonian cameraman his final shot for the film. ❦

(A version of this article appeared in *Smithsonian Folklife Festival 1998*.)

The Wisconsin Dairy Farm: A Working Tradition

by Ruth Olson

Head milker Carrie Dassow makes her rounds at the Rau family farm in Dorchester, Wisconsin.

"The culture of dairy farming pervades the state. . . . Many still value such connections and credit farm life with providing strong family ties, moral instruction, and a sense of stewardship of land and animals."

Wisconsin boasts a population of 1.45 million dairy cows. That's one cow for every three people. With more than 27,000 dairy farms, we produce almost 15 percent of the nation's milk, 25 percent of its butter and 30 percent of its cheese. Clearly, the state still deserves the title "America's Dairyland."

Clark County shares with neighboring Marathon County the honor of having the largest number of dairy cows in the state, 62,000 cows each, give or take a few. Clark County is the picture of a healthy farming community, its landscape dotted with working farms and agriculture-related businesses, feed cooperatives and implement dealers, pole barn construction companies, and milk pick-up stations. You're likely to meet a milk truck on any of the county's small rural roads and just as likely to come across tractors pulling whatever piece of equipment is appropriate to the season.

The culture of dairy farming pervades the state. Many residents either grew up on a farm or spent time on the old "home farm" run by relatives. Many still value such connections and credit farm life with providing strong family ties, moral instruction, and a sense of stewardship of land and animals.

Photos by Andy Kraushaar

Winter light passes through the curtain of the free-stall barn on the Boon family farm in Greenwood, Wisconsin; (inset) a Wisconsin classic, the Holstein.

But most people rely on an image of farming from the past rather than actual knowledge of what farming looks like in the 1990s. Contemporary dairy farming demonstrates a principle folklorists love to pronounce: culture, like the traditions that assist in its maintenance, is dynamic. It changes to suit the needs of the members of a particular community at the same time that it retains the core values of that community. While farms are becoming much larger and technologically more complex, they are still community-based and resource-conscious. Most are still family concerns.

More and more contemporary dairy farms feature a milking parlor, where the cows enter stalls to be milked and then are released into return lanes to head back into the adjacent barn. The milker stands in a pit about three feet lower than the milking stalls, where he or she can easily put the milking machine on the cow without having to bend over.

Many farms now have free-stall barns, long, open one story structures where the cows wander in large pens, entering stalls to eat or lie down. These barns have cur-tained sides that can be raised in the summer to allow a breeze to pass through. Most farms still keep their old two story barns but find new uses for them, frequently as treatment barns for sick cows or mothers ready to give birth.

Near the milking parlor or in the house you'll find the farmer's office, filled with certificates and awards, pictures of cows and kids, an aerial view of the farm, and, of course, a computer. All the information on each cow's breeding records, health records, and milk production are on computer now, and that computer may be hooked up to the Internet, allowing the farmer to participate in agriculture-based discussion groups, nationally and within the state.

Where Dick and Peggy Rau run their 700-cow farm near Dorchester in Clark County, there's a lot of community support for dairy farming. Peggy says, "We don't meet a lot of people who are against us. You'll meet a few people who say, 'Oh, you're putting the little farmer out of business.' Well, not really. What would the difference have been if we would have stayed at seventy-two cows? We'd just be struggling the same as the rest of them, and I'd probably

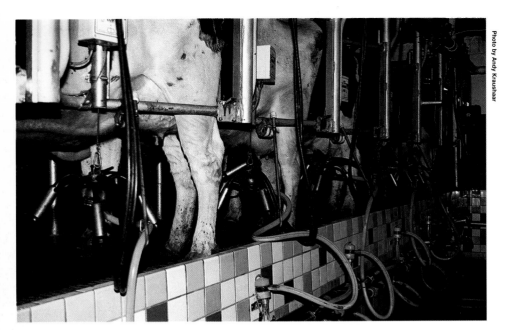

The Boons laid all the tile in the pit of their new milking parlor.

have an off-farm job instead of staying here. I've been lucky enough to be here eighteen years, and I've never had to work off. I've always been here when the kids leave and when they get home, which I consider a big plus."

The heart of the family farm remains its children. The family always hopes that the farm will be there for the children who want to continue the tradition. So farming has to be more than just financially secure; it has to be something the children can imagine themselves doing. Expanding the farm helped increase the kids' interest in farming, Peggy Rau says. Son Zack helps to maintain the cows' feeding schedule, getting up at four in the morning to help feed. A year ago daughter Stephanie began working as a milker, and Peggy and Dick have been surprised by her enthusiasm. "Who would have ever thought she'd be talking to her friends about cows?"

Part of what makes their current mode of dairying attractive is that, with an expanded work force, it's now possible to leave the farm now and then. "When we milked seventy-two cows, you had to be here at five in the morning, five at night, and now, like Steph's basketball game tonight, we just go, that's it," Peggy marvels. "We get done what we have to get done, and then we leave. A big plus." Dick and Peggy can take every other weekend off, and for their anniversary

last year, they flew to the Packer game in Florida. "We never did that in the first fifteen years we farmed," Peggy notes. "We never left."

Not everyone who grows up on a farm continues to farm, of course, but many go into related businesses. Dick's brother, for example, is with Northstar Breeding Service, where Dick and Peggy buy most of their semen. Peggy's brother works for Marawood Structures, which put up the Rau's newest free-stall barn.

Farm life still centers on relationships with animals. Although there may be hundreds of cows, they are not faceless and nameless. The older cows, especially, become pets. Peggy describes how her milkers develop friendships with certain cows. Their milking parlor has a basement below it which also serves as a storm cellar. One day last summer Peggy was warning her milkers to get down to the basement in any severe storm. She told them, "Forget the cows, just get yourselves down there." Her head milker asked, "Can I bring 1459 with me?" All the milkers feed cookies, cupcakes, and chips to another cow, 1541. One milker suggested to Peggy that since they mix bakery waste as part of the cows' integrated feed program, it was the same thing as feeding the cows cookies anyway.

Most farms still adhere to the old principle, "Find a use for it." The original recyclers, farmers put old things to work in new ways. For example, Duane Boon of Greenwood in Clark County recently expanded his herd to 120 cows and bought a milking parlor system. Rather than build a whole new operation with all new buildings, Duane modified his existing round-roof barn. He gutted out one end of it, air hammered out the floor to install the pit for the milking parlor, and changed the gutter system and stanchion setup in the other end to create a holding area for the cows waiting to be milked. He connected his new free-stall barn to his old barn, so the cows can be moved from one location to the other easily.

Sometimes old ideas fit new purposes. In Dick and Peggy Rau's milking parlor pit, all the stuff needed to prepare the cows for milking—towels, teat dip, sanitized water—used to be kept in a barrel, and the milkers would have to run back and forth to get supplies. Then Dick's brother welded together a trolley, much like an old silage cart, suspended from a track on the ceiling. Now the milkers simply pull the trolley along as they milk.

Farmers have always needed to adapt equipment or create new equipment to fit specific working environments. A new version of the lowly manure scraper provides an example.

A neighbor found that old tractor tires cut in half make the perfect manure scraper for a free-stall barn. Using a metal bucket to scrape the concrete floor causes two problems: first, it eventually smooths out the floor too much, making it slippery for the cows; second, metal buckets scraped against concrete wear out rather quickly and are expensive to replace. Using an old tire is cheaper and better for the floor.

The Raus, like other farmers in the area, buy their tractor tire scrapers from the local farmer who makes them. This specialized market emphasizes how much dairy farmers rely on a healthy, supportive environment. Few dairy farmers operate successfully in isolation.

Many of the family farms that go out of business every year were owned by older farmers. Those farms get absorbed by other farms, since not many new farmers can afford to start up. "Like my dad said, I'm farming right now what basically was ten independent farmers thirty years ago," Duane Boon says. "It's kind of sad in a way."

Peggy Rau shares Duane's attitude. "As far as the farms being active, that's always the sad part for me. I like the old farms . . . I happened to go sit out in the woodlot one day, and you could see around this area, how many people are sixty, sixty, sixty, sixty." She points around her to her neighbors. "Dick's brother farms right up the road half a mile, so that one's running. The farm over there with the green silo top, another big farmer that lives out on A owns that, and there's hired people going through it constantly, so it's really not a family-run farm anymore. That farm over there is currently running, but not for long."

Farmers are well aware of the risks they take in this rapidly changing business, but for families like the Raus and the Boons, the risk increases their determination to pass on workable traditions.

Before they expanded, the Boons milked sixty cows, and did all right, "but I came to the point where I'm forty years old," Duane Boon says. "If I keep milking sixty cows, my net worth will probably go down by the time I'm sixty. I either have to modernize and expand, get out, or just milk it out till there's nothing left. I've got kids coming up, I think they might be interested. Maybe not. If not, I've got to have something saleable, too."

At the Raus, Dick's uncle, a retired farmer, says, "I remember when I was milking twelve cows. I thought I'd be a big success if I could get it up to thirty cows. By the time I retired, I was milking seventy, and now. . . ." He gestures behind him at the complex that milks and cares for 700 animals. ❧

(A version of this article appeared in *Smithsonian Folklife Festival 1998.*)

> *"Farmers are well aware of the risks they take in this rapidly changing business, but for families like the Raus and the Boons, the risk increases their determination to pass on workable traditions."*

Photo by Andy Kraushaar

A special pen keeps these Holstein calves warm on the Rau farm.

Wisconsin Remains Polka Country

by Richard March

The nineteenth-century European immigrants to Wisconsin arrived with polkas ringing in their ears. The polka, a lively couple's dance in 2/4 time, had emerged from its folk roots to become a European dance craze in the 1840s. In elite Paris salons and on humble village squares and taverns, polka dancers flaunted their defiance of the older staid dance forms, the minuets and quadrilles that had preceded this raucous, scandalous new dance.

The same historical and social upheavals that produced the polka also launched thousands of European villagers on their uncertain and perilous migration to the American Midwest. They became farmers, miners, lumberjacks, factory workers, and entrepreneurs in the new land, but they continued to enjoy the music and dance traditions of their old homelands, passing them on to the American-born generations.

The booming popularity of brass bands coincided with the emergence of the polka. Innovative tinkerers in France, England, and Germany developed a new family of instruments—accordions and concertinas—based on the principles of the *sheng*, a Chinese free reed instrument, but using the levers and springs of the Machine Age. As the electronic keyboard was in the late twentieth century, the squeeze box was the nineteenth century's most popular mechanical instrumental innovation. A single musician could replace a small ensemble, playing melodies and harmonies on the right hand while the left hand produced rhythmic chords and bass notes. A button accordion or concertina became the prized possession in many an immigrant's pack, and that musician undoubtedly played a lot of polkas.

Upon arrival in Wisconsin, the polka became an American folk tradition. At rural

Photo by Andy Kraushaar

Cletus Bellin and his orchestra perform Czech-style polka music at the Polka Festival, Norman, Wisconsin.

ABOVE: Marty Nachreiner and son at rehearsal in Trempealeau, Wisconsin.

LEFT: Karl Hartwich plays Dutchman-style polka and is recognized as an outstanding concertina player of his generation.

house parties with the rug rolled up or at corner taverns in industrial towns, a squeeze box or a horn kept the neighbors' feet stomping out polkas.

A variety of American polka styles evolved in different sections of the Midwest, shaped by the creativity of particular talented and influential musicians. The styles have ethnic names—Polish, Slovenian, Bohemian, Dutchman—based on the origin of the core repertoire and the ethnic heritage of many of the musicians. But in the Midwest, ethnic groups share the music and dancing, and most bands are ethnically mixed.

In the twentieth century, radio broadcasts and recordings spread the polka to new enthusiasts. Clear channel WCCO in Minneapolis broadcast Whoopee John's Dutchman music to six or more states, much as WSM's Grand Ole Opry spread Southern traditional music. The recordings of groups like the Romy Gosz Orchestra and Lawrence Duchow's Red Ravens aided their efforts to become popular as regional touring dance bands.

Right after World War II, almost exactly a century after the original polka craze in Europe, polka music and dancing briefly entered popular culture in a big way once more, this time in America. Slovenian American accordionist Frankie Yankovic became the biggest star, and his style attracted devotees nationwide. Lil' Wally Jagiello's recordings on his own Jay Jay label established Chicago as the center for the

Polish polka style and converted many musicians to his "honky" sound.

By the 1960s, rock 'n' roll had captured the popular music industry, but polka has endured in a variety of grassroots folk communities, where polka musicians and dancers have organized institutions to perpetuate their passion. A network of polka dance halls, clubs, festivals, newsletters, mail order recordings outlets, accordion makers and dealers, and radio and television shows covers the country.

Four of Wisconsin's fine ethnic polka bands illustrate the range and impact the polka has had on the state.

Karl Hartwich: Portrait of "one flying Dutchman."

Karl Hartwich was born in Moline, Illinois, in 1961. His father had relocated about 200 miles down the Mississippi River from his hometown near La Crosse, Wisconsin. He was seeking a well-paying factory job making agricultural implements in the Quad Cities area. But farming was in his blood, so the Hartwich family lived outside of town in rural Orion, Illinois, where they raised hogs and field crops.

Karl was raised in Illinois, but his family didn't lose touch with their Wisconsin relatives. Karl remembers that at least twice a

Photo by Bob Rashid

Dancers at the Riverview Ballroom in Sauk City, Wisconsin, pass on the vitality and fun of the polka tradition.

month they made the trek upriver to attend dances where his distant cousin Syl Liebl and the Jolly Swiss Boys were playing. Liebl, a Dutchman-style concertina player, is a natural musician, inventive, spontaneous, passionate, and original. Little Karl must have absorbed the style.

In response to his pleas, Karl received a concertina as a Christmas present at the age of twelve. A few months later he was sitting in with the Swiss Boys, and six months after that, at age thirteen, he had his own band, which is now in its twenty-fourth year. Karl has turned out to be just as inventive and passionate a musician as his mentor. The concertina is always on his mind. Karl recalls driving the tractor on his family's farm, with dance tunes ringing in his head, the engine roaring, his left hand on the wheel, his right hand on the tool box beside the seat pressing out concertina fingerings on the vibrating metal.

Karl has moved back upriver to Trempealeau, Wisconsin. Virtually every weekend he packs up the van and instrument trailer, and he and his sidemen converge on a dance hall or outdoor polka festival. Casual in his dress and personal style, Karl is nonetheless very serious about his music. He's recognized as the outstanding Dutchman concertina player of his generation. Paradoxically, his music is at once controlled and free. Karl has added more syncopation, chromatic runs, and improvisa-

tional flourishes to his play than any of his predecessors but adheres to the basic tenets of the Dutchman style.

When not playing music Karl loves living on the river and is an avid fisherman. Between his band's dance gigs, he catches Mississippi River catfish on treble hooks baited with chicken livers, then fillets and fries the catfish to perfection.

Cletus Bellin speaks Walloon, plays Czech.

Cletus Bellin, a proud member of the Walloon Belgian ethnic community of northeastern Wisconsin, is also the leader of one of the finest Czech-style polka bands in the Midwest. A proficient pianist and a very strong singer, Cletus learned the correct pronunciation of the Czech language lyrics from a friend in the nearby town of Pilsen.

As a boy in the 1940s on a southern Door County, Wisconsin, farm, Cletus was as likely to speak the Walloon Belgian dialect of French spoken in his highly culturally retentive community as the English he learned in school. Cletus has had a lifelong interest in his Belgian culture and, now in his 50s, is one of the area's youngest remaining fluent speakers of Walloon.

Cletus has played in the Wisconsin Bohemian- or Czech-style bands of Marvin Brouchard and Jerry Voelker and worked for many years as the radio station manager and on-air personality for a Kewaunee, Wisconsin, polka station. Moved by the style of singing and play of the Czech musical performing groups Budvarka, Veselka, and Moravanka, which toured Wisconsin in the early 1980s, Cletus resolved to start his own band performing in a style closer to the European manner from which the Wisconsin Bohemian bands had diverged. His group is widely acclaimed at polka festivals and Czech ethnic events throughout the country.

Steve Meisner accepts his father's challenge: polka music must be all or nothing.

Steve Meisner was born in 1960 in Whitewater, southwest of Milwaukee. At the time, Steve's father Verne was already an established musician, an accordion prodigy whose original band, Verne Meisner and the Polka Boys, was aptly named. The members were still in their early teens when they started taking professional gigs. That was the early 1950s, just in the wake of Frankie Yankovic establishing the Slovenian style of polka as one of the most popular forms of music in Wisconsin. By the 1960s, the Verne Meisner Band was one of the best known polka groups in the region.

When at age seven Steve began entreating his father to teach him to play, Verne at first rebuffed him. Then the father thrust a momentous decision on his young son: "If you begin to play, you have to promise that you'll never quit."

Steve leapt at the challenge. Only a year later his father began to bring Steve along to play some jobs with the Meisner band, often placing the diminutive kid on a box so he could reach the microphone.

Steve started his own band while still in his teens and has continued the family polka tradition, playing regionally and nationally, producing his own CDs and videos, and organizing polka tours and cruises. Steve acknowledges his musical debt to the Slovenian-style musicians of the previous generation but has pushed the form in hot arrangements and in original material expressing a range of emotions.

The Happy Notes of Norm Dombrowski.

When Norm Dombrowski was a teenager in the 1950s, he wasn't particularly inspired by the polka bands active in his hometown of Stevens Point, Wisconsin, a rural area of central Wisconsin populated by Polish American dairy and potato farmers. The Dutchman style of polka was popular at old-time dances. According to Norm, the bands he heard didn't sound too lively or spontaneous. Perched behind bandstands, the musicians seemed to keep their noses buried in their sheet music.

In 1956 Chicago's Lil' Wally Jagiello gave a legendary performance for two nights at the Peplin Ballroom in Mosinee, just north of Stevens Point. Huge crowds turned out. Norm heard a modern Polish polka sound firmly grounded in the Polish folk music familiar to him from house parties and weddings. He was impressed because there was no sheet music, and the band was very lively, reminiscent of rock 'n' roll bands.

Norm decided he wanted to play in this style and to become a singing drummer, like his new hero, Lil' Wally. By 1960 he was able to start the Happy Notes Orchestra with three friends, playing for dances locally and as far afield as Minneapolis and Chicago.

The Happy Notes evolved into a family band as Norm's children grew old enough to be competent musicians. Unlike most other Polish-style bands, Norm did not adopt the modern, so-called "Dyno" or "Push" style, remaining closer to Lil' Wally's "honky" style of music. Norm stresses the singing of the old Polish songs but also includes German, Czech, and Norwegian numbers to satisfy patrons of other ethnic backgrounds.

These four polka practitioners, each with a different musical style, indicate how vital the polka traditions remain in Wisconsin. ❦

(A version of this article appeared in *Smithsonian Folklife Festival 1998*.)

". . . polka has endured in a variety of grassroots folk communities, where polka musicians and dancers have organized institutions to perpetuate their passion."

Norm Dombrowski and the Happy Notes strike a pose before they strike up a polka.

The Water Always Calls: Occupational Endurance and the Life of Daniel "Pete" LeClair

by Michael J. Chiarappa

"It is as much of a calamity to lose the fishermen as it is to lose the fish. Fishing communities around the world have harbored the ways of the sea in themselves, a knowledge not soon acquired again after it, and they, have been abandoned."

John Hay, *Desertion of the Fishes*

When you cross eastward over the East Twin River on the Seventeenth Street Bridge in Two Rivers, you encounter two views that evoke the community's long history of commercial fishing.

The southern view reveals the looming constant, Lake Michigan, which started calling Two Rivers commercial fishermen to its fishing grounds as early as the 1830s. To the north, along the banks of the East Twin

River huddle the fish tugs, storage sheds, processing buildings, nets, docks, trap net boats, and fish boxes that enabled generations of Two Rivers fishermen to harvest Lake Michigan's waters.

This section of Two Rivers still functions as one of the workplaces of Wisconsin's few remaining commercial fishermen, including Daniel "Pete" LeClair. Born on June 28, 1929, Pete LeClair grew up in what may have been the most highly-charged

Pete LeClair works at the smelt sorting machine at the Susie-Q Fish Market, Two Rivers, Wisconsin.

Photo by Michael J. Chiarappa

The LeClair's fish tug **Susie-Q** *at the wharf outside LeClair's fish market.*

"Early on, LeClair recognized that family cooperation provided commercial fishing with its needed daily energy, and, more subtly and gradually, supplied inherited knowledge of fishing techniques and fishing grounds."

maritime environment in Wisconsin. Located at the base of the Door Peninsula, Two Rivers contained, along with its commercial fisheries, the well-known marine manufacturing operations of the Kahlenberg Brothers Company (marine engines) and the Carron Net Company (gill nets, pound nets, trap nets, and seines). The region surrounding Two Rivers supported an established boat building tradition, including the Burger Boat Company in Manitowoc and, at Sturgeon Bay, the Peterson Boat Works and the Sturgeon Bay Boat Works.

Numerous other participants in this region escape formal documentation—men working in small machine shops and foundry works, women mending nets in barns and basements, and families constructing and repairing boats in their backyards.

Early on, LeClair recognized that family cooperation provided commercial fishing with its needed daily energy, and, more subtly and gradually, supplied inherited knowledge of fishing techniques and fishing grounds. When LeClair assumed his place in his immediate family's working rounds, he also took his place alongside the larger

LeClair clan and other Two Rivers fishing families with French Canadian roots.

LeClair came of age as a fisherman with Two Rivers firmly identified as Wisconsin's commercial fishing center. During the 1930s and 1940s, LeClairs and LaFonds from Two Rivers represented commercial fishing interests in Wisconsin commercial fishing organizations, the Wisconsin Conservation Commission, and the Wisconsin State Senate and Assembly.

LeClair's memories of his family's involvement in the region's commercial fisheries begin with his great-grandfather Charles LeClair's descriptions of tending pound nets with rowing and sailing skiffs, in the days when lake trout, whitefish, and herring were plentiful.

Pete LeClair's line of the LeClair family began commercial fishing in Two Creeks, about ten miles north of Two Rivers. "I was ten or eleven years old and I used to drive truck (a 1929 ten-ton Chevrolet flatbed) for my dad while he worked with the nets in the fields," LeClair recalls. "I've been in it since I was old enough to really work or be useful for something."

One of the oldest surviving fish storage and processing buildings in Two Rivers.

LeClair soon graduated to hauling the "crib" or "pot" section of the pound net by hand from an open pound net boat. The pound net is a stationary net device, held in place by stakes. It catches fish by directing them into the holding area, known as the "crib" or "pot." Relying on stakes to hold them in place, pound nets were suitable in the Great Lakes region's shallower waters with mud or sand bottom. But that also made them susceptible to serious damage or outright destruction from ice flow. This created the substantial maintenance burdens through which young Pete received his introduction to the fishery.

The dockside yield of lake trout, the prime catch of Joseph LeClair's fishery, became increasingly unstable, prompting changes in LeClair's early fishing experience. During the late 1930s and early 1940s, Joseph LeClair began the transition from pound net to gill net fishing. As Pete LeClair recalls, this change meant more than just switching from one type of netting technology to another.

Gill netting—nets that stand vertical in the water by floats and weights and catch fish by the gills as they attempt to swim through—is the most flexible of all commercial fishing methods used on the Great Lakes. This harvesting method allows fishermen to pursue a greater number of species at greater distances from shore, at greater depths and in more locations. But these options require watercraft that can handle these environmental conditions and the vast amount of netting to be set and pulled, and onshore facilities for storage and preparation space for the netting and fish catch.

For Joseph LeClair, this led to the acquisition of the wooden fish tug *Margaret*, a boat Pete remembers as testing his family's ship carpentry skills. "My dad [had] to put in all new boards and redo the whole hull," LeClair recalls. "They had big oak frames, and I remember them soaking them and trying to bend them to fit the hull." At this time, the elder LeClair also moved his storage building from Two Creeks to the Two Rivers location adjacent to the current LeClair fishing operation.

During the 1940s, the steel fish tug became increasingly popular among Great Lakes fishermen. LeClair says his father didn't share this enthusiasm. Instead, in the mid-1940s, he worked closely with Swartz Marine in Manitowoc to design his new steel fish tug. He wanted a boat with greater stability. Joseph LeClair's new *Susie-Q* had a more angular hull while keeping the ice-breaking capabilities of a more curved bow.

Joseph LeClair impressed on Pete that survival in Wisconsin's Lake Michigan fisheries required innovation and experimentation. These thoughts accompanied Pete in 1952 when he and Bill Kunesh bought the fishery from his father. Referring to the 1950s as "some pretty tough years," LeClair remembers the ecological disaster of sea lamprey predation of lake trout and whitefish. "You would fish these gill nets, and the lake trout would just rot and lay on the bottom," he remembers. "Lots of our nets we never got back because the leads on the bottom would sink through the decayed trout. When you tried to pull it up, you would get your ropes back, but your web would be gone. You couldn't pull it out of the decaying lake trout on the bottom."

In 1962, after fishing with gill nets for ten years, LeClair changed the way he fished. Prompted by the state's urgings to thin Lake Michigan's excessive chub stocks, LeClair adopted trawling, a harvesting technology well-established on the Atlantic,

Pacific, and Gulf Coast but hardly known on the Great Lakes. The trawler drags a large, funnel-shaped net from a vessel's stern. This new course guided LeClair's fishing activity until 1991.

The adoption of trawling technology gave Wisconsin's commercial fishermen a chance to pursue alewife, smelt, and, to a lesser degree, chub, in greater volume for new markets. It also required the fishermen to expend a great deal of effort and capital in adopting a saltwater fishing technology to freshwater conditions. LeClair acknowledges that trawling is as much a skill as it is a technology. "In '62, we didn't know a trawl from, you know. . . .," LeClair admits.

Through his own observations and experimentation, coupled with constant dialogue with the Marinovich Trawl Company in Biloxi, Mississippi, LeClair gradually developed a trawl suited to the conditions and target species of Lake Michigan.

A fisherman's success with a trawl net depends on how efficiently he can set, drag, and lift the net. Having worked with trawl nets for over thirty years, LeClair notes that you acquire such knowledge only gradually, by working with the nets. His first efforts with a trawl were less than spectacular. "We started with this old small *Susie-Q* and I'll tell you we didn't have much money to buy a trawl net at that time," he recalls. "It was $1,500 I believe. We went out the first day and we lost her. Got a shipwreck and lost the whole works. Went out the next day, lost another one. So then we got hold of an old car ferry captain who had been on the lake a long time, and he had a map of all the lake's shipwrecks. He also had a map explaining the lake bottoms, the rocks, the reefs, and where the clay balls were. We worked with him for several weeks and marked out an area where we had a good sand bottom where we had a halfway chance. This developed into the fishery," he concludes, "and the only way you do it is through experience."

LeClair trawls a very small portion of Lake Michigan, an inshore area ranging five miles east and ten miles north of Two Rivers. He understands this lake bottom and fish habitat well. LeClair and his fellow fishermen began refining their use of the trawl net, which only operates as effectively as a

fisherman's ability to keep it open and moving with minimum resistance at appropriate depths. Two large rectangular pieces of wood, called "doors," attached to the "wings" (the net's open end) keep it open during dragging. LeClair developed rigging and engine arrangements to allow him to effectively reel the net's cables and fish loads on his particular boats, and he spent countless hours determining how to get the most effective net spread from the trawl's doors by selecting the best angle for the doors to move through the water.

"If it's going 45 to 50 degrees, it's not good," he reports. "If it goes to 33, you're in the ballpark where you'll get an excellent spread and pull the easiest. This is all done from our own trial and error, experience and time, lots of wasted time."

LeClair worries about the future of such fishing methods. "Once all this knowledge is gone, you know, if somebody doesn't continue this," he warns, "it's not ever going to come back, because nobody's ever going to do what we did. . . . You can't take them out of the street and throw them in your boat. My kids started from high school . . . straight on through, and so did these other fishermen from other families that fished on the lakeshore. They all learned from their dads. And now these

"Joseph LeClair impressed on Pete that survival in Wisconsin's Lake Michigan fisheries required innovation and experimentation."

Smoked Great Lakes fish awaits customers in LeClair's Two Rivers market.

The heirloom photos displayed in LeClair's market serve to remind us of the great tradition and heritage of Great Lakes commercial fishing.

people, their kids, they're not growing up with family tradition."

The LeClair fishery now faces significant limitations on the time it's allowed to trawl, further complicating matters. The boats need to average two-and-a-half to three knots to keep the net on the bottom, although they can go faster if the fish are swimming in shallower water. As trawling time is curtailed, it becomes more difficult to sustain boat handling skills, along with the ability to adjust and patch nets. "You take a long, long time to get these captains experienced on the operation of the net, the equipment, where to fish and so forth," LeClair stresses.

Trawlers can't turn quickly. A captain must be able to compensate for the tug's delayed response. LeClair recalls a number of close encounters with large vessels that failed to heed his radio warnings.

Of all the adjustments LeClair made to make trawling feasible, none are as prominent as those he required to enable his tugs to lift and store heavy net loads. Great Lakes fish tugs are designed for working gill nets. Lifting a trawl bag full of smelt or alewife over the boat's stern can have disastrous results if not handled properly.

When he first started trawling, LeClair used the family's first *Susie-Q*, a relatively small fish tug at thirty-five feet long and eight feet at the beam. While the *Susie-Q's* size limited her storage capacity, her low stern freeboard (the distance between the water and the top of the bulwark) caused LeClair greater concern. When lifting the trawl bag on board, the stern descended so far, the *Susie-Q* took on water.

LeClair worked with two machinists from Hilbert, the Krueger brothers, to develop a stern ramp and reeling drum that would safely lift his nets. But even with these improvements, the *Susie-Q* still labored under the cumulative weight. "There's only that much freeboard here," LeClair notes, "so they would put the ramp on, and the boat goes down and you get twenty thousand pounds of fish on the back end and pretty soon you're going to take on water. We almost sank a couple of times."

Realizing that the problem was the size of his boats, not the stern ramp technology, LeClair started acquiring the larger fish tugs used by his family fishery today. In 1962 he acquired the *Avis J*, and in 1972 he replaced the older *Susie-Q* with a new boat bearing the same name. Both of these steel fish tugs measure fifty-five feet by sixteen feet.

"You can pull up twenty-five or thirty thousand pounds at one time right into the boat," LeClair notes.

During the 1970s and 1980s, the LeClair operation focused on alewife, smelt, and chub for the pet food and fish meal markets. These boats produced a state record when they harvested 250,000 pounds of alewife in a single day. Such large hauls were unloaded by an augur device that directed the fish to an elevator, which, in turn, transferred the catch to a tractor-trailer.

Even with all these innovations, LeClair's family continues to use some of the old methods as well. Gill netting for chubs involves six-foot high nets lifted after three days. Net maintenance is less demanding since the shift from cotton to nylon, LeClair notes, but fishermen still have to retain skill in hanging net—the process of connecting the mesh to the maitre lines that hold the floats on the top of the net and weights on

"LeClair's love of his work resonates for all who enter his working world."

the bottom. While pursuing chub, fishermen will set as much as two-and-one-half miles of gill nets. Mechanical net lifters eliminate the burden of hand lifting, but, LeClair notes, to safely retrieve the nets and fish, captains have to be skilled in maneuvering their fish tugs while doing simultaneous tasks. Workers clean the chubs carefully while the tugs return to port, to maintain quality when the chubs are smoked.

During the past five years, the LeClair family has also started using trap nets (submersible nets that function similar to pound nets) to catch whitefish in the spring.

The LeClair's onshore facility consists of a number of buildings and a wharf along the East Twin River. The LeClair fishery is known locally and in broader marketing circles as the "Susie-Q Fish Market," although they do more than sell fish there. The wharf itself consists of substantial steel bulkheading and fuel storage that allow the *Susie-Q* and *Avis J* to unload their catch and refuel. The LeClair fishery's workshop and storage building, fish processing building, and smokehouses are next to the wharf. Throughout and around these buildings you find the tools of the fishery trade: a smelt sorting machine, a smelt fillet machine, net drying reels, fish smoking racks, storage boxes, and trap net anchors.

Rather than conform to modern smoking methods, which rely on gas and wood

chips, the LeClair family smokes fish the traditional wood fire way, using hardwood logs of maple, apple, and beech to obtain the regionally-known flavor of smoked Great Lakes fish. Wood storage sheds surround the smokehouses so the fires can be gradually increased and maintained. The fish market fronts the street, farthest from the wharf. While the aromas of the smokehouse are enough to set the LeClair fishery apart, it's also one of the few remaining in the Great Lakes region where every operation associated with the occupation occurs.

Occupational identity and tradition are observed and upheld here. A collective spirit unites all who work. They value their work, its history, and the bonds it fosters with the water and its resources.

In his office, LeClair keeps photographs of all his fish tugs. On the front of the Susie Q Fish Market, a carved sign depicts a fish tug with a stern ramp for trawling, a symbol of the fishing technology that so defines Pete LeClair's life. Inside the market hangs a photograph of the *Susie-Q* dramatically breaking ice in the East Twin River, and a scale model of the same boat perches on a shelf behind the counter. These items chronicle the family's and community's fishing history and celebrate an occupation that engages three generations of LeClairs.

Although he turned the fishery over to his oldest son, Michael, in the 1980s, Pete is still integrally involved in the fishery. His experience and understanding make him the inspirational leader and elder statesman of this fishing family. Michael exhibits the same commitment to the fishery, as do his brothers, Paul and Daniel. Michael's wife, Kathy, and his daughter, Jamie Ann, also work in the family business.

Still, the LeClair patriarch worries. "When my kids are gone," he reflects, "there's nobody coming up after them. We are the last family of LeClairs that fish out of Two Rivers. Where there used to be eighteen boats out of Two Rivers, now we are down to two." LeClair's love of his work resonates for all who enter his working world. All who value the Great Lakes commercial fisheries echo his love and honor his endurance. ❧

Voices for the Heart: Traditional Hmong Marriage Negotiation

by Mai Zong Vue

A Hmong house can be a busy place when a wedding is being planned, with a complex, multigenerational conversational dance. But the most important conversation occurs between the *mej koob*—the marriage negotiators. Two people sit on each side of a small table in the living room. The four *mej koob* (pronounced "may kong"), two from each family, get acquainted, establish rules, ameliorate past disputes, negotiate the dowry price, and, ultimately, celebrate the wedding.

You'll find four or five *mej koob* per Hmong community in Wisconsin. The role they play in bringing a couple together in marriage has grown from centuries of tradition almost as old as the first Chinese empires.

Being one of the few *mej koob* in Madison, Wisconsin, Kou Xiong is in great demand, handling almost every Hmong wedding in Madison, four or five per year. "I travel all over the state and even out of state sometimes," Kou says. He has performed more than forty weddings since he became a marriage negotiator. "When everyone keeps turning to you every time they need you, you run out of excuses for rejecting them," he admits, "so you keep on doing the job."

Kou acknowledges that *kev tus siab*—a mixture of peer pressure and obligation—plays a big part in his decision to continue to help the community.

"When people see that you possess the skill, they will ask for your help," he says. "If you decline, they will feel that you are self-ish, may be mad at you, and may never ask for your assistance again. It is important to help others with what you know because you will depend on others to help you, too."

Kou's life began in the mountains of Laos near the borders of China and North Vietnam. He was born to the peaceful farming community of the Hmong, one of sixty ethnic minorities found in Laos. The Hmong had never encountered the West before this century, living an idyllic, simple existence in the mountains. His life, like many others, was deeply affected by the fighting that took place during the Vietnam War as his people were drawn into the "Secret War" supported by the CIA to disrupt the Ho Chi Minh Trail.

Photo by Mai Zong Vue

Dang Yang of Milwaukee displays the qeej, *a traditional Hmong instrument. Hmong refugees who settled in Wisconsin are keeping their customs, from music to marriage negotiations, alive in their new communities.*

When America withdrew support for the Royal Lao government and the rest of its commitment to Southeast Asia in the early 1970s, the Hmong were soon targeted by their former enemies for brutal reprisals, turning them into refugees who would soon be scattered across the world to Australia, Thailand, French Guyana, France, Canada, and the United States. Many would never see their families again.

Like many Hmong, Kou arrived in Wisconsin in 1980 and has been in Madison almost from the beginning of his resettlement. Kou was one of the lucky ones, finding strong support for himself and his family in Wisconsin. He has helped others adjust to life and resettlement in Wisconsin as well.

He became a *mej koob* in 1981, after shadowing a few weddings and learning the proper marriage procedures from his uncle Fa Dang Xiong, an expert *mej koob* from La Crosse. Kou started with being the helper for the marriage negotiator twice and observed three different marriages prior to practicing by himself.

Despite holding a full-time job and managing a four-unit rental apartment, Kou enjoys helping the Hmong community, and being a *mej koob* is one way of contributing.

"An advantage of being a *mej koob*," Kou says with a smile, "is that you do the talking and let others drink."

According to Kou, there are two types of wedding rituals in the Hmong custom. The most common is the *tshoob tog qws* or regular wedding. The second, *tshoob zawj*, is a wedding "by request or influence of family and relatives," Kou explains. *Tshoob zawj* is traditionally required when the groom's parents ask the bride's parents for their daughter's hand in marriage for their son, perhaps using clan money and status to influence the bride's parents. The *tshoob zawj* rarely occurs in this country, Kou explains, due to cultural adaptation.

The regular *tshoob tog qws* is needed when the bride and groom like each other and consent to the marriage. It also comes into play for *zij* or "taking of the bride." One of the most confusing aspects of Hmong culture, *zij* revolves around the idea that, although the bride likes the groom, she wants to appear to dislike him to help the family

Photo by Kou Xiong

In preparation for a Hmong wedding the bride's marriage negotiators offer a toast to the groom's negotiators. These negotiators or **mej koob** *play a vital role in the wedding tradition.*

maintain honor. *Tshoob tog qws* also applies when a widow or divorcee remarries or the marriage is forced under circumstances.

Each wedding has thirteen key participants:

Two *mej koob* or marriage negotiators from each side

The bride and the groom

The *tus tais ntsuab* or bridesmaid and the *phib laj* or best man

Two parents, one from each side

Two *nus tij* or brother by relation

One *txwj laus* or elder

The *tshoob zawj*, or marriage by request or influence, also requires a *tus txhiaj com*, who must know all the wedding procedures even better than the *mej koob*, a daunting challenge indeed.

The two *mej koob* serve as messengers and negotiators. Parents will use the grapevine to warn each other of bad marriage negotiators—those who take the wedding as an opportunity to abuse alcohol and those who deliver inaccurate messages between the parents.

The bride and groom play a minor role in the Hmong wedding. The groom plays the bigger role, standing before the bride's parents and relatives to take his oath to love

"You'll find four or five **mej koob** *per Hmong community in Wisconsin. The role they play in bringing a couple together in marriage has grown from centuries of tradition almost as old as the first Chinese empires."*

Origin of *Zaj Tshoob:* Dragon Wedding

Long, long ago, four young boys walked toward the woods to hunt. Each possessed a special talent—one was a swimmer, one a fortune-teller, the third an archer, and the fourth a healer. As they were walking, the fortune teller told his friends, "In a little while there will be a bird flying."

Soon they saw a bird flying. The archer took his bow and arrow and shot the bird. The bird was hurt in one wing and fell into the pond. The swimmer quickly took his shoes and shirt off and went to get the bird. When the swimmer reached the bird, it had become a beautiful woman. He brought the woman to shore. The healer quickly brought the woman back to life.

The woman was Ntxawm, a princess of the water dragons. The princess chose the swimmer to marry, and they prepared to conduct the wedding with her father, the King Dragon. The princess Ntxawm told them that in order for her father to acknowledge them, they must speak their words in songs. If they did not sing, there would be no wedding. So when the bride and groom, two marriage negotiators, the bridesmaid and best man arrived, the marriage negotiator began to sing. For a long time there was no answer.

As the singing ended, the Dragon King opened the door and welcomed them, "Who are you? What brings you to my house? Come in and we will talk."

The Dragon King was overjoyed that the Hmong had rescued his daughter and knew how to speak his language. The Dragon King gave his blessing for the wedding, held a big feast, and everyone celebrated the good news.

Ever since then, the Hmong have sung for the Dragon King for their weddings on earth. That's why the wedding song is called *Zaj Tshoob* or dragon wedding.

(Note: Yong Kai Moua is a clan leader living in Eau Claire, Wisconsin. He told this legend at the Hmong Youth Conference in Wisconsin Dells in August of 1997. He in turn heard the legend from his grandfather, Txwj Kawm Muas, when the elder was still alive.) —M.Z.V.

The *phib laj*, or best man, accompanies and supports the groom throughout the wedding and often assists in the wedding ritual.

The parents are usually represented by a brother or uncle of the bride's father and the older brother or distant relative of the groom's father. They act as the parents by listening to the parents' advice and decisions. The parent from the groom's side will also be responsible for managing the financial matters and wedding issues assigned to him.

The two *nus tij*, or older brothers by relation, welcome the groom by taking off his back basket, the blanket, and the lunch upon arrival. Upon the return, the two *nus tij* bring their back basket, the blanket, and lunch outside for them. Certain penalties apply if the *nus tij* do not fulfill their roles.

Kou notes that back in China, the *nus tij* will also play the *qeej* to welcome the groom and bride home, but this ritual is no longer practiced in America.

The *txwj laus*, or elder, oversees the wedding ceremony from beginning to end. This elder doesn't have to know all the wedding rituals but manages the wedding.

The *txhiaj com*, or master of marriage negotiator, is only needed for a marriage by request or influence. He guides the four *mej koob* to be fair throughout the wedding.

The mej koob *conducts eight steps upon arriving at the bride's house:*

1. *Tsabyeeb.* To initiate conversation with the bride's parents, the *mej koob* offers cigarettes to the head of the household and whoever is there and asks for the clan leader. If the clan leader is far away, the *mej koob* uses the telephone. Often, the distant clan leader will delegate wedding preparations to someone else.

2. Introduction of the four *mej koob.* Once the two *mej koob* from the bride's side have arrived, they pull a table in the living room with four chairs, a bottle of rice whiskey, and white wine or beer, and the four negotiators bond, set rules and get to know each other.

3. Check of *fi xov.* In *fi xov*, the bride consents to the marriage and leaves with the

the bride. The bride's role is to take care of the groom if he gets drunk and to be a resource for the groom's aide. For example, if the groom's side doesn't know her father's relatives, she'll direct them to the appropriate individuals.

The *tais ntsuab*, or bridesmaid, accompanies the bride to secretly guard her so she doesn't reconnect with her ex-boyfriends and to make sure the bride's mother doesn't try to change the bride's heart (which usually happens when the wedding is by request).

groom to his house. The groom's side sends two people to notify the bride's parents of the bride's whereabouts so they won't be worried. In this first step in the marriage negotiation, the *mej koob* from the groom's side asks if *fi xov* was conducted appropriately. This is the time for the bride's parents to bring up any wrongdoing and penalize the groom's side if necessary.

4. Check of aunt and uncle. The *mej koob* must check for any outstanding arranged marriage or engagement with the *phauj* and *yij laug*. If there is an existing engagement or arranged marriage, the negotiators must resolve the issue before proceeding by consulting with the groom's parents and carrying out their wishes carefully.

5. Interclan issues. This is the time for the bride's parents to bring up marriage concerns, if any, between the clans and to build a stronger bond to ensure a healthy marriage. According to Kou, this often generates a lot of heat and can often lead to cancellation of the wedding if there are many unresolved disputes between the two clans.

6. Proposing the dowry price. The dowry negotiation is the last step before the actual wedding feast. The groom's family must supply a small amount of money as collateral, guaranteeing that the groom and his clan will not abandon and abuse the bride. Usually, the wedding gifts that the bride's parents and relatives give to her are much more than the dowry price.

7. Wedding preparation and the actual feast. The bride's parents can prepare the wedding feast or give it to the groom's side. The *mej koob* of the groom's side asks if the *mej koob* of the bride's side would like a green pig (cash) or a white pig (actual pig). In a traditional wedding in Laos, the pig must be six *taus* or approximately thirty-two inches and usually must be a male. The pig is sacrificed for the celebration. Food, drinks, and laughter fill the room at this stage. The gifts for the bride to begin her new life are read off to the two *mej koob* from the groom's side, and a written marriage contract is presented to the *mej koob* of the groom's side.

During the wedding feast, toasts salute the new life. The toasting can take up to five

A traditional Hmong necklace is often worn by wealthy brides. Made of silver, the jewelry is a symbol of prosperity.

hours, depending on the size of the bride's family and extended family members.

8. *Tiam mej koob* or thanking of the marriage negotiators and key players. After the wedding feast, when the bride and groom have returned to the groom's house, the groom's parents put together a *tiam mej koob* feast for all the players in the wedding. The *mej koob* report back to the parents on the contracts, gifts, and wedding process. The parents then thank each individual who devoted energy and time in carrying out the wedding and give a small amount of money to signify their appreciation.

Hmong marriages are a celebration of community and the deep bonds of kinship. The practice conforms as closely as possible to the ways of the ancestors in ancient China while adapting to new options available in America. Some families and clans still request a very traditional wedding, while others accept a simplified wedding. For example, while some Hmong families instruct the *mej koob* to sing every wedding song, including songs to set up the table, to accept the umbrella, and to invite guests to eat, others let go of this small ritual to shorten the wedding process.

As a wise *mej koob*, Kou pays very close attention to the parents' wishes. ❧

Cheeseheads, Tailgating, and the Lambeau Leap: The Green Bay Packers as Wisconsin Folklore

by Robert T. Teske

> *"The Packers' long and celebrated history, replete with star players and great coaches, stirring victories and stinging defeats, has enhanced the aura of tradition surrounding the team and supported the creation of popular heroes who still capture the imaginations of football enthusiasts everywhere."*

Madison fans gather at a Lambeau Field tailgate party in anticipation of a Green Bay Packers game.

I've been a Green Bay Packers fan all my life. When I attended Mother of Good Counsel Grade School on Milwaukee's northwest side during the late 1950s and early 1960s, my brothers and I watched the Sunday afternoon telecasts of the Packers games and then rushed out into the backyard to imitate the heroics of Paul Hornung and Jim Taylor, Bart Starr, and Ray Nitschke.

Later, when my size and lack of speed transformed me from a sandlot quarterback into an offensive center at Marquette University High School, I would go to almost any length to see the Packers play. One of my fondest boyhood memories is of scaling the corrugated steel wall behind the scoreboard at Milwaukee County Stadium before the annual Shrine Game between the Packers and the Bears, only to be greeted by several hundred Shriners preparing to take the field for pregame ceremonies astride horses, bicycles, and miniature motor scooters. Their superior numbers and trusty mounts notwithstanding, my good friend Rex Lowe and I would not be denied: we leapt to the ground and ran like hell for the old right field extension, where we lost ourselves in the gathering crowd and watched the game from a carefully chosen vantage point near the concession stand.

Several years later, as a freshman at Harvard University, I picked the lock on my proctor's door to watch my beloved Packers trounce the Kansas City Chiefs in Super Bowl I, winning a bet from Kansan David Achtenberg, who lived across the hall. Super Bowl II produced another stirring Packer victory.

The following year, as a junior on the 1968 Harvard varsity, I found myself in distinguished company. Tommy Lee Jones, then Al Gore's roommate and more recently one of the country's top box office draws, started at guard for the Crimson. I played a small role, snapping for punts and extra points, throughout most of that season, including the Harvard-Yale game. While I treasure my memories of college teammates and fabulous finishes, as a Packers fan, I recall the Super Bowl victories of the preceding seasons almost as clearly.

Little did I know during those heady championship seasons that almost thirty years would pass before the Packers would return to the Super Bowl. A generation of Packer fans would have to suffer through humiliating losses to the likes of the Chicago Bears and the hated Dallas Cowboys. My own son would be a senior in college before the Green and Gold would reclaim the Lombardi Trophy they brought back to "Titletown" following Super Bowls I and II.

Yet, throughout this long drought, during which I found myself moving to Philadelphia, Detroit, and Washington, D.C., before returning to Wisconsin in 1985, I remained a committed Packers fan—and so did literally millions of others. Why such loyalty? Why such dedication and commitment?

The answers to these questions lie, I think, in the success of the Green Bay Packers in appealing to Wisconsin's appreciation for tradition, community, and celebration—the same sentiments that have supported the rich and diverse folklore and folklife of the Badger State over its 150-year history.

For more than seventy-five of those 150 years, the Packers have been a vital part of Wisconsin life. While other professional sports franchises found their way to Milwaukee starting in the 1950s, the Braves,

The famous post-touchdown "Lambeau Leap" is demonstrated by a Packer to the delight of this section of fans.

the Brewers, and the Bucks, despite world championships in their respective sports, have never commanded the fan support of the long-established Packers. Such dedication and commitment takes time to develop; identification with a team and pride in association require stability as much as success. Only the Packers have endured long enough to inspire the handing down of season tickets from one generation to another as bequests in family wills.

The Packers' long and celebrated history, replete with star players and great coaches, stirring victories and stinging defeats, has enhanced the aura of tradition surrounding the team and supported the creation of popular heroes who still capture the imaginations of football enthusiasts everywhere. Fans from my father's generation recall the likes of Curly Lambeau, Don Hutson, and Buckets Goldenberg, while

LEFT: Packer fans who aren't fortunate enough to possess tickets still enjoy tailgating and watch the game on a television they brought to the parking lot of Lambeau Field.

BELOW: Packer quarterback Brett Favre prepares to take the snap from center Frank Winters.

people my age compare such legendary figures as Vince Lombardi, Bart Starr, Willie Davis, and Willie Wood with their contemporary counterparts Mike Holmgren, Brett Favre, Reggie White, and LeRoy Butler.

Moments like Bart Starr's quarterback sneak to secure a last minute "Ice Bowl" victory for the Packers over the Cowboys on the "frozen tundra" of Lambeau Field must now share the team's highlight film with Desmond Howard's punt return for a touchdown in Super Bowl XXXI. No matter which plays or players Packers fans regard as the best, each new game adds to the tradition, the lore and legend of Packer football.

Sense of community plays a role as important as tradition in securing a place for the Packers in the hearts of Wisconsin fans. As the only publicly-owned National Football League franchise in the United States, the Packers enjoy a unique affiliation with the smallest market in professional sports. However, the Packers' ties to the community are far closer than any ownership documents could suggest. Every player who borrows a bike from a local kid for the daily ride from the locker room to the preseason practice field strengthens his connec-

tion to the community. So does every player who makes the "Lambeau leap," joining the fans in the stands after scoring a touchdown.

The Packers don't belong to Green Bay alone. The team's fan support extends throughout America's Dairyland and well beyond. For games in Tampa Bay, for example, many "snowbirds" who have fled Wisconsin's winters for sunny Florida gather with other loyal fans to generate a crowd of some 30,000 Packer backers. Cities like San Francisco and San Diego, despite having their own professional teams, typically have at least one bar designated as a gathering place for area Packer fans. Only the Fighting Irish of Notre Dame enjoy the support of fans so widely distributed around the country, making the Green and Gold truly "America's team."

In addition to building a formidable tradition and cultivating a broad-based community, the Packers have long been the occasion for, and center of, Wisconsin celebrations. Packer parties extend from the preseason in July till the last second ticks off the clock during the Pro Bowl in late January. Schools and businesses regularly hold "Green and Gold Days" before big games, and merchants host autograph signing sessions.

But the central Packer celebration remains the one that engulfs Lambeau Field during every Packer home game. In much the same way that Cheese Days in Monroe give local dairy families a cause to celebrate and *Syttende Mai* in Stoughton encourages members of the Norwegian community to get together, Packer games are a celebration for those attending, and even those watching the game on television or listening on the radio.

Clothed in the ubiquitous "cheeseheads," construction hard hats decorated to resemble Packer helmets, Packer jerseys, Packer jackets, and green and gold face paint, Packer fans arrive hours before game time to take part in a form of revelry known as "tailgating"—cooking bratwurst on charcoal grills in the Lambeau Field parking lot, washing down the sauerkraut-covered sausages with another venerable Wisconsin product, beer, and throwing a football around. After the game, a trip to the local tavern to review the highlights may well be

Photo by Andy Kraushaar

in order. A Packer game provides a full day of celebration.

With their victory over the New England Patriots in Super Bowl XXXI, the Packers demonstrated that, as bumper stickers had proclaimed hopefully, but prematurely, for years, "The Pack Is Back." Had they also beaten the Denver Broncos in Super Bowl XXXII, they would have been "Back to Back."

Whether good fortune continues or another thirty-year dry spell ensues, the Green Bay Packers will remain an essential part of Wisconsin because of the team's abiding tradition, its ability to create community, and the occasion it provides for celebration. ❧

(A version of this article appeared in *Smithsonian Folklife Festival 1998.*)

Sporting an array of game day attire, Packer fans love gathering for a tailgate party at Lambeau Field, Green Bay, Wisconsin.

You Can Get Anything You Want at La Tienda San Jose

by Craig Stinson

In the old downtown district of Whitewater, Wisconsin, sandwiched between a restaurant and bar and across the street from an old bank, stands the San Jose Mexican Store. Stucco, painted a light brown, covers the brick, making it look like adobe, the earthen building material used in much of Mexico. In the window signs in both Spanish and English announce that the store is "*abierto*/open." You've found La Tienda Mexicana San Jose. Most people just call it "San Jose" or "La Tienda"—the store.

Whitewater lies at the northern part of Walworth County in southeastern Wisconsin, almost exactly in the middle of the triangle created by Madison, Milwaukee, and Chicago, Illinois. Milwaukee has a higher number of Latinos, but Walworth County has the highest percentage of Latinos of any county in Wisconsin. Most recent immigrants have come to work in the service and tourism industries around Lake Geneva. They learned about jobs through networks of friends and family. In the northern part of the county, where Whitewater is located, most recent immigrants from Latin America work for General Motors cars or Trek bicycles or in food canneries.

Like the central and eastern Europeans who immigrated to Wisconsin in the late 1800s, the people from Latin America bring their languages, their music, their food, and their desire to make their new land home.

Tienda San Jose has been open at its present location for five years. The owners, Rafael and Ana Rodriguez, are both from Mexico. Rafael, 29, was born and raised in Mexico City. He came to Delavan, Wisconsin, in 1984 and then to Whitewater in 1988, where he worked in a General Motors manufacturing plant. Ana, 26, is from the small town of San Jose de Otates in the state of Guanajuato, about five hours northeast of Mexico City. They have three children, ages two, five, and six, all born in Wisconsin. When not in school, the children often play in and in front of the store.

Around 90 percent of the business for Tienda San Jose comes from the local Mexican and Mexican American community within a thirty mile

Photo by Craig Stinson

La Tienda San Jose in Whitewater, Wisconsin, offers a wide selection of videos to rent; the majority are in Spanish, or if not, they have Spanish subtitles.

Photo by Craig Stinson

La Tienda San José owner Rafael Rodriguez attends to a telephone call while ringing up sales at the cash register.

radius, Rafael says. The other 10 percent is from the local Anglo American community, including students from the University of Wisconsin -Whitewater. Spanish dominates in the store.

Tienda San Jose is a mixture of stores found in Mexico, serving as grocery, butcher shop, and restaurant, and as music, video rental, and clothing store. Most of the products in the store are Mexican. For example, although Wisconsin is known all over the United States for its cheeses, Rafael and Ana stock their store with "Supremo" brand cheese from Chicago. Supremo makes Mexican cheese for quesadillas (two tortillas with cheese grilled between them), soups, chili *rellenos* (stuffed chili peppers) and other needs specific to making good homestyle Mexican foods.

Other foods not found in a supermarket include *nopales* (cactus leaves, minus the stickers!), the *tamarindo* (tamarind, a fruit with a sour and sweet taste used mainly in candy and as a drink), and chili *colorado* (a dried red chili used for seasoning with meals). You can also buy *pan dulce* (Mexican sweet bread) or other candies imported from Mexico, like *Pelon Pelo Rico* (a tamarind candy whose name translates "good-tasting bald guy" because you push the candy up through holes on the top of its plastic container to make it look like hair that you eat), candies with chili peppers, and *membrillo* (an apple-like fruit made into a thick jelly).

Folks need something to drink with their food. While Coca-Cola and Fanta are popular, *"Jarritos"* ("little jars") is probably the best known soft drink imported from Mexico. Flavors include pineapple, tamarind, and guava. My personal favorite is an apple-flavored soft drink called *Manzanita*, or "Little Apple." Tienda San Jose also serves as a music store where one can buy cassettes and CDs by artists from all over Latin America. One of the largest selections of music is Mexican *norteño* (northern style), dance music driven by a polka beat, with an accordion and brass instruments. The store stocks groups like Los Tigres del Norte (The Tigers from the North), Bronco, and Los Huracanes (The Hurricanes).

Photo by Craig Stinson

The shelves at La Tienda are packed with food and goods, from chilies and cheese to T-shirts and CDs, most of which is produced in Mexico. While many store patrons are Anglo Americans, the majority of customers are from Mexico and have strong ties to their homeland and its products.

"The informal network of friends and information at La Tienda helps members of the Mexican community negotiate the intricacies of their new home."

Classic *ranchera* artists include Antonio Aguilar and Mexican mariachi singer Vicente Fernandez. The latest in rock 'n' roll from Latin America includes the Caifanes, a Mexican band that opened for the Rolling Stones in Mexico City a few years back; Shakira, a Colombian singer invoking pop beats with reggae; Los Fabulosos Cadillacs (The Fabulous Cadillacs), an Argentine ska, salsa, and reggae band that did a great version of "Strawberry Fields Forever" with Deborah Harry from Blondie; and the always fun Mexican band, Café Tacuba.

T-shirts hanging from the ceiling bear silk-screened images of low rider cars, U.S. and Mexican flags, and even Emiliano Zapata, the hero of the Mexican revolution, with his famous phrase "I would rather die on my feet than live on my knees." Other shirts feature the Virgin of Guadalupe or the patron saint of Mexico and Aztec carved figures. You can also get leather jackets, boots, and belts with "Mexico" and decorative motifs carved into the leather.

The large video selection at La Tienda includes many of the latest Hollywood blockbusters with Spanish subtitles and a great selection of movies from Mexico.

"Golden Age" Mexican films include movies by the beloved Pedro Infante and the classic comedian Cantinflas. More current offerings include the critically acclaimed *Como Agua Para Chocolate* (*Like Water for Chocolate*) and the 1970s series about a Mexican wrestler, Santo, who fights famous monsters like Dracula, the Wolfman, and *Las Momias de Guanajuato* (*The Mummies from Guanajuato*).

The restaurant looks like the small, roadside restaurants found all over Mexico and serves some of the best Mexican food north of the Rio Grande. Red and white checkered plastic cloths cover the tables and bear a salt shaker (no black pepper), slices of Mexican lemons or small limes, and a bowl of homemade salsa, either red or green, depending on the type of tomatoes used. The plastic bowl looks like the real stone *molcajete* in which one grinds the ingredients for salsa.

The first time I ate at the restaurant, a person eating at another table turned to me and said, "Watch out for the burritos." Gesturing with his hands, he said, "They're this big. One will fill you up." I ordered *gorditas*, which are similar to a sandwich made with pita bread. They are made with thick tortillas, either corn meal or flour, sliced open for a filling. Tienda San Jose makes its *gorditas* with *rajas con queso* (chili peppers with cheese), *carne* (beef), and *frijoles* (refried pinto beans).

Not heeding the warning I had received, I ordered three, expecting them to be small like ones sold in Mexico. They were the size of hamburgers, and I finished a little more than one before I had to ask for a bag so I could take the rest with me. Ana told me they had originally made them smaller, but complaints forced them to prepare them bigger so people "feel like they're getting their money's worth."

The food at Tienda San Jose is a lot different than Mexican food found in Mexican-owned restaurants catering mainly to a non-Mexican population. At La Tienda, where the business comes almost exclusively from people from Mexico, ties to the homeland are strong, and the menu includes tacos made of beef, *tripa* (cow intestine), pork and cow tongue, and *menudo* (a soup delicacy made of cow intestine, chili peppers, and hominy). You can also get *tortas*, Mexican-style sandwiches made of French bread toasted in the oven and filled with lettuce, tomato, jalapeños, onions, and various meats and cheeses.

The restaurant also serves as a meeting place. People from the local Mexican community get together to talk about their jobs, complain about their bosses, and find out what's happening at home (Mexico and

The restaurant at La Tienda San Jose offers a gathering place for the local community and a menu that includes gorditas with rajas con queso, homemade salsa, and many other Mexican specialities.

Whitewater), how the kids are doing in school, and what's happening over the weekend. They take time out to be among people who speak the same language, are intimate with the culture, and understand the difficulties of adjusting to a new climate, political system, economy, and culture.

The informal network of friends and information at La Tienda helps members of the Mexican community negotiate the intricacies of their new home. Rafael and Ana are quick to tell people where to find jobs and housing and where to take a car to get repaired.

An immigrant confronting a completely new life finds comfort here. La Tienda Mexicana San Jose offers everything one might need and cannot find elsewhere: food, information, music, clothing, videos, and company. ❧

Our Own Thumbprint In It: How Dickeyville Created the Grotto

by Anne Pryor

When the glaciers bypassed south-western Wisconsin, they left behind beautiful rolling hills, hidden valleys, rocky bluffs, multiple rivers, and caves. Bordered by the Mississippi River and Iowa on the west and by Illinois on the south, this former lead mining region is today farmland and cheese making country.

In the southern Grant County town of Dickeyville, a constructed wonder rivals the natural richness of the area: the Dickeyville Grotto, a masterpiece of folk architecture.

Photo by Anne Pryor

Built from 1919 to 1930, the grotto honors the land through its display of rocks and minerals indigenous to the upper Mississippi region. It also honors the religious and patriotic beliefs of its builders.

The Dickeyville Grotto is actually a series of rock and embellished concrete structures spread over the grounds of Holy Ghost parish. "Embellished concrete" means that during the building process, when the concrete was still damp, it was decorated with patterns of colorful shells, stones, glass, petrified moss or wood, and geodes.

The grotto began with a memorial group and a Eucharistic altar in the cemetery, then grew in stages with the addition of a grotto dedicated to the Blessed Mother that sits in center place between the church and rectory; a shrine dedicated to Christ the King immediately behind that; a shrine built to revere the Sacred Heart of Jesus behind the parish school; and, at the western edge of the property, the large patriotic shrine that honors the American ideals represented by Columbus, Washington, and Lincoln. Flower gardens with decorative railings connect the separate shrines into a grotto park.

The creative visionary behind the grotto was Father Mathius Wernerus, a German immigrant missionary priest who was pastor of Holy Ghost parish in Dickeyville from 1918 until his death in 1931. When Father Wernerus immigrated to Wisconsin from the Rhine province of Germany in 1904, he brought the European Catholic custom of erecting outdoor grottoes and roadside shrines dedicated to

A series of shrines, gardens, fountains, and sculptures made of stone and embellished cement can be found at the Dickeyville Grotto in southwestern Wisconsin.

The spire of Holy Ghost Catholic Church rises above the grounds of the Dickeyville Grotto.

ilies, her own included, taking turns with their horses and wagons hauling the huge rocks that had been sent by train. Henry Melssen remembers his father, Leo, a blacksmith, making all the iron railings for the garden fences that Wernerus then decorated with embellished concrete. He also recalls that the Holy Ghost parishioners supplied most of the money for the construction projects.

Many current parishioners recall with pride the items their families donated for the grotto. George Busch can point out the rocks that came from his family's farm. Parish members proudly gave porcelain figurines, kitchen crockery, ceramic bowls, and glass dishes, even though money was scarce in those post-Depression years.

Berning tells of being a young girl during the construction of the Blessed Mother's grotto. Father Wernerus needed money for two stained glass windows in the interior of the grotto. As Berning tells it, "Father said one day, 'Anybody like to donate a window?' I had won ten dollars at the Labor Day picnic, and of course we were very poor because my mother was blessed with six kids. I couldn't hardly get to school fast enough that next morning with my ten dollar bill. I gave one [window] and Elizabeth Hesseling gave the other one."

The children of the parish were involved in other ways as well, providing them with wonderful memories of the grotto. Current elders such as Henrietta Hauber, Busch, Melssen, and Berning recall being called out of school to help Father Wernerus with different tasks. In a 1995 interview, Joe Salzman told of how the nuns at the Holy Ghost school sent misbehaving children to Wernerus as punishment. "He'd put us to work out here or in the house, or

"Dickeyville elders believe that the process brought the people of the parish together, giving them a common purpose and a special identity as collaborators with Wernerus on this uncommon communal project."

favored saints. Wernerus adapted this Old World tradition to the American Upper Midwest, probably inspired by the grotto construction and technique of another German missionary priest, Father Paul Dobberstein, the builder of the Grotto of the Redemption in West Bend, Iowa.

The Dickeyville Grotto is Wernerus's monument to his religion and his country; he called it "Religion in stone and Patriotism in stone."

Father Wernerus could not have realized his architectural dreams without support and assistance from the Holy Ghost parishioners and residents of Dickeyville, two groups that were just about synonymous in the 1920s. These German and Dutch Catholic farmers helped him in innumerable ways, according to current parish elders who were children during the grotto's construction. Esther Berning remembers parish fam-

Photos by Anne Pryor

TOP PHOTO: *The Corpus Christi altar is an important part of parish annual processions.*

BOTTOM PHOTO: *Other grottoes in Wisconsin, such as the Holy Family Grotto in St. Joseph (near La Crosse), are part of a larger grotto tradition reflecting religious and patriotic values and themes. The Holy Family Grotto was also built during the 1920s and 1930s.*

his housekeeper would give us some candy. It wasn't bad to be sent there."

Hauber remembered that she washed rocks and helped to "put things together." Berning remembered how she helped to decorate the concrete. "He had a six by six little box without a top on and he'd put cement in there and when that cement was partly set then we'd help put that colored glass in that cement," recalls Berning. "That's how come it's so colorful. . . . We were honored if we were sent over here to help from school. It was great."

Everyone who could be recruited helped Father Wernerus wash rocks. Girls tended to help with the embellishment, especially working with Father Wernerus's cousin and housekeeper, Mary Wernerus. She did much of the work with colored glass, creating wonderfully fanciful embedded glass flowers. Boys tended to help more with heavier tasks such as carrying rocks or, in the spring, carrying out the decorated cement pieces that Father Wernerus had built in his living room or church basement over the winter. "That was the amazing part, you know," Hauber recalls, "that he'd do that all in the house in the winter, no pattern, no nothing, and they'd take it out and then it would fit."

Dickeyville elders believe that the process brought the people of the parish together, giving them a common purpose and a special identity as collaborators with Wernerus on this uncommon communal project.

In a lovely case of history repeating itself, a similar experience occurred when the parish, under the direction of then pastor Father James Gunn, restored the grotto. In 1995 a man visiting the grotto was so moved by the sculptures that he offered to help restore them. As grotto manager Marge Timmerman explained, the visitor happened upon the grotto while visiting the university in nearby Platteville. After touring the grotto, he was convinced, "God has been so good to me and my construction business that I feel He led me here."

The visitor donated the labor of his construction crew during the summer of 1996, and the parish supplied materials and money. While the professional crew led the

The "Tree of Life" design appears of the back wall of the grotto.

Photos by Anne Pryor

A heart-shaped design of cement embedded with seashells makes a decorative fence for a grotto garden.

restoration effort, parishioners again volunteered their labor after Father Gunn put out a call for helpers. So many people volunteered, Timmerman said, "sometimes there was almost too much help."

Gunn put a box outside his rectory door so parishioners could donate crockery, housewares, porcelain, special rocks, and minerals—items just like those the earlier generation of parishioners had donated in the 1920s. Even though the grotto's storage shed was filled with boxes of unused materials left over from Wernerus's own collection, Gunn solicited new donations to create future memories. He wanted the current generation of parishioners to be able to point with pride to what they, their parents, and their grandparents had contributed in 1996 to this collective effort. At Gunn's direction, incorporating the newly donated items into the grotto during the restoration took precedence over use of the original materials.

Gunn also made sure to include the parish children in the restoration process, just as Wernerus had done. For Father Gunn, this was an important way for the current youth to develop the same strong ties to the grotto held by their elders. "People have the pride, especially with the young people that take a part in this," Father Gunn reflected. "So it's not something that somebody else did but it's something that I had a hand in as well. As we say around here, we like to have our own thumbprint in it as well."

The parish members have had their "thumbprint in it" in other ways as well: parishioner governance of the grotto, scrupulous care of the gardens by artistic parish volunteers, fund raising that includes a summerlong church basement garage sale, and by parish teenagers serving as tour guides to the 60,000 annual visitors.

The chance to participate in the grotto's reconstruction afforded a wonderful opportunity for current parishioners to join earlier generations as cobuilders with Father Wernerus, making the Dickeyville Grotto "memory in stone" for many Dickeyville residents. ❦

(A version of this article appeared in *Smithsonian Folklife Festival 1998.*)

Goodness Gracious! For Local Flavor and Fellowship, You Can't Beat a Church Supper

by Terese Allen

"The Wisconsin calendar is filled with Lutheran lutefisk dinners, Catholic fish fries, and Greek Orthodox banquets, all offering a feast of homemade regional specialties plus a large helping of camaraderie."

I spent a great deal of my youth at St. Willebrord's, four blocks from our home in the center of Green Bay. At St. Willie's I endured the frequently dragging hours of grade school and daily Catholic mass. Even time spent on the playground, where I joined in perpetual games of marbles and king-of-the-mountain, could get tedious. But one event at St. Willie's, was a highlight in my young life—penny suppers.

I loved these monthly parish potlucks, held in the school's basement. The experi-ence started with the scent of coffee greeting us at the front door and hovering in the hallways. This was not today's coffee, not an in-your-face dark roast gourmet brew. It was a kinder, gentler cafeteria coffee that bub-bled in tall, shiny percolators big enough to blow a fuse if you plugged two into the same outlet. I was too young to drink that coffee, but I drank in its smell, which signaled "spe-cial occasion."

The scent led down a dim staircase and into the big hall set with rows of long tables.

Photo by Andy Kraushaar

At the Nativity Blessed Virgin Mary parish dinner in Tisch Mills, Wisconsin, booyah *and smelt are the specialties. Popularized by Belgian immigrants,* booyah, *a thick and rich soup of chicken and vegetables, is wonderful when made in a huge outdoor cauldron.*

Here the rules were suspended. The crowd was a noisy jumble of families, friends, nuns and priests, the evening a carefree interval with no assigned seats, no lessons to recite, no sermon to sit through. We kids got away with things unheard of during the school week: streaking and sliding across the gleaming linoleum floor, even romping in the spooky underground tunnel that connected St. Willie's school to its church.

Best of all, we could eat whatever we wanted from the buffet tables. They filled quickly with jiggly Jell-O salads, tuna noodle casseroles, and various Tater Tot-topped ground beef concoctions—bland dishes, yes, but in enough variety to awe a 10-year-old with limited dining out experience. Still, the budding foodie in me held out for the really good stuff: slow-cooked crocks of bubbly, crusted-over baked beans, hand-kneaded whole grain bread, and the dishes that I would only later recognize as "ethnic," specialties like pork chops and sauerkraut and the bumpy, cream-filled pastries we called "kneecaps."

Such heritage foods were the best part of the church suppers of my youth.

Today, touted in the latest cookbooks and at upscale restaurants, this type of heartland cooking is all the rage. But for those in search of a true taste of the region, you won't find it in a glossy cookbook. For the real thing, the place to go is still a church supper.

The Wisconsin calendar is filled with Lutheran lutefisk dinners, Catholic fish fries, and Greek Orthodox banquets, all offering a feast of homemade regional specialties plus a large helping of camaraderie. If you think of them as somewhat dated, small town socials, think again. While you'll still find old-fashioned value and fun at each, today's church-sponsored meals—not all of them technically "suppers"—come in all shapes, sizes, locations, and seasons, and they serve their communities as fund-raisers for parish projects, as volunteer opportunities, and as carriers of community identity and tradition.

As I travel the state, I'm always on the lookout for these low-key, low-priced repasts. Luckily, one of my favorites is not far from home: the annual Pork Hocks and

Lutefisk—a traditional dish of cod treated with lye, soaked in water, boiled, and served with butter—is served proudly at a dinner at Vermont Lutheran Church.

Sauerkraut Supper, an incredible spread of traditional German specialties held at St. James Catholic Church in Madison.

"The Kraut Feed," as it's sometimes called, is held in late February or early March. Dinner organizer and head chef Emmett Schuchardt serves a menu that hasn't changed since the meal started more than thirty years ago: meaty Canadian pork hocks simmered in stock, home-fermented kraut seasoned with caraway, boiled potatoes, rye bread, and cream-style corn. If pig's ankles sound challenging, there's also smoked sausage or wieners. Homemade desserts,

beer, and other beverages round out the meal.

Schuchardt says the supper menu reflects a time "when people worked with wheelbarrows and shovels, when people had to eat." It also reminds diners of the church's ethnic roots, which were so strong during the parish's earliest years that sermons were given in both German and English.

"My sister, Phyllis Schuchardt, was the one who would make it a German day," Schuchardt recalls. "The whole deal: flags, posters, place settings. For years a high school band would play German music. But now it's getting away from the German thing." These days whimsical handcrafted pink pig centerpieces instead of German flags adorn the dinner tables, and the only truly German American particulars at the event are its menu items and a number of the older diners and volunteers.

What was once primarily a celebration of heritage is now a coming-together of a diverse urban community. St. James' multicultural churchgoers, however, aren't the

The hosts proudly wear clothes reflecting their Norwegian heritage (top photo) while guests at the lutefisk dinner at Vermont Lutheran Church near Black Earth enjoy the fare (bottom photo). A Norwegian dinner might include lutefisk, lefse (a potato crepe), meatballs, and a variety of buttery pastries.

Church and community suppers are a big but rewarding project. Volunteers—young and old, male and female—pitch in to get the job done. Behind the scenes volunteers work together at the lutefisk dinner at Vermont Lutheran Church, and at a great many such traditional suppers and dinners throughout Wisconsin.

only participants. In a town of many diversions—including more restaurants per capita than just about any city in the nation—St. James' old-time banquet lures the general public, too. Hundreds accept the challenge of German style pork hocks.

While ethnic cooking is a draw for diners at St. James, to parishioners of St. Hagop's Armenian Church in Racine, it's also a symbol. *Madagh*, a rich, long-simmered stew of lamb or beef, is the centerpiece dish at an annual picnic held in Johnson Park. *Madagh* is also the name of this event, observed in memory of Armenians killed in 1915 by the Turkish government. The descendants of those who survived and immigrated to Wisconsin gather to cook, bless, and share the traditional stew. In doing so, they honor and preserve their heritage and celebrate their community.

"People come from near and far," says Julie DerGarabedian, an active member of the church. "They plan their vacations around it."

Madagh and its accompanying grain dish, a nutty bulgur pilaf, are prepared over a smoking pit in immense pots lined up to look like a miniature Manhattan skyline. And they, too, are a symbol; servers dish the meal from these communal pots family style, highlighting the value the St. Hagop community places on sharing.

The sharing goes further. There is no charge for the meal, but diners make donations to support the church and its programs. Some of the stew is saved for neighbors who are homebound or in nursing homes. Picnickers contribute traditional foods brought from home, foods like cucumber yogurt salad and pita bread. And, as at St. James, the public is encouraged to participate in, and learn from, this celebration of heritage.

"Our church is a close-knit warm family," DerGarabedian says. "You can really feel that warmth extended to Armenians and non-Armenians as well."

Church suppers have been providing hospitality like this since early in Wisconsin

"Rarely advertised outside parish bulletins and local weeklies, church-sponsored meals are fueled by word-of-mouth and repeat business. Regulars, nourished by the comfort food and friendliness they encounter, wax enthusiastic about the unique pleasures of each event."

history. In *The Flavor of Wisconsin* (University of Wisconsin Press, 1981), author Harva Hachten suggests that Wisconsin's first church fair was held in 1835 or 1836, when the Green Bay land sales office was selling the newly platted communities of Milwaukee and Navarino. Wanting to mark the occasion, "women of all denominations got together to raise money. There was a church supper of great quantity and much variety." Whether or not this was the first, certainly communities have been producing such meals ever since.

Rarely advertised outside parish bulletins and local weeklies, church-sponsored meals are fueled by word-of-mouth and repeat business. Regulars, nourished by the comfort food and friendliness they encounter, wax enthusiastic about the unique pleasures of each event. According to one older gentleman who frequents meals in and near Dane County, "Every one has their own specialty. St. John's in Waunakee has homegrown lettuce. St. Bernard's in Middleton does different salads—everybody brings their favorite. At Lodi it's Swiss steak. And have you been to the fish fry at St. Peter's in Ashton? They have that homemade bread. Dane has a fish fry with, what

do they call those? Fritters. But, oh, I like that homemade bread at Ashton."

It takes a small legion of laborers to make such an event happen. Who prepares the crowd-sized recipes and cleans the mountains of dirty dishes? Volunteers, of course.

At the kraut feed it's chiefly senior citizens who peel the potatoes, slice the bread, and serve the beverages. For weeks before the Armenian picnic, parish ladies prepare authentic specialties like stuffed grape leaves and Armenian pastries, to be sold from food booths during the event. Older parishioners, especially women, are often the ones with the time and expertise to produce a banquet, but don't be fooled by any stereotype of a dinner volunteer. In Westby, at an annual dinner given by Our Savior's Lutheran Church, for example, men provide a feast that feeds 800.

And it's no simple preparation. Since the majority of Our Savior's congregation is Norwegian American, nothing but lutefisk and *lefse* will do, plus meatballs, mashed potatoes, rutabagas, coleslaw, coffee, and a variety of Norwegian butter pastries.

Lefse is a kind of potato crepe. Lutefisk—a traditional dish of cod treated with lye and soaked in water, boiled, and served with butter—is more of an acquired taste. "It's different," admits Pastor Gary Dames. But nobody is complaining at Our Savior's. "People come from as far as the Twin Cities. One winter, when it was thirty to forty degrees

Photo by Anne Pryor

Slavski hleb *is a special decorated bread made in honor of saints' days for celebrations at St. Sava Serbian Orthodox Cathedral in Milwaukee.*

Grade school volunteers pose for the camera before launching into dessert preparations for the St. James Catholic Church "Kraut Feed" in Madison.

below zero, more than five hundred still showed up."

Why do male parishioners manage this meal? "Why not?" muses Pastor Dames. He says members of a church group called the Men of Our Savior started the meal in 1988, "strictly as a fellowship, not a fund-raiser." It's grown considerably and now "the money is good, too. It supports church projects. It's a way to get the men involved. And the women don't have to worry about all the cooking and serving."

Community service is a heartfelt value to these volunteers, and they pass this and other values on to youth at Our Savior's by involving them in the dinner, too. Children learn how to make traditional cookies like *sandbakkels* and rosettes and help serve the meal. They gain a sense of responsibility and teamwork and of the history of their parish. "We pass on the tradition," Dames says.

The more things change, the more they stay the same? Traditional Wisconsin church suppers prove it. St. James is no longer a

"German" parish. You won't find women washing the dishes at the lutefisk dinner in Westby. At St. Willebrord's, my old stomping grounds, the grade school has been torn down, the tunnel is gone, and Saturday night masses, aimed at the parish's Latino population, are now offered in Spanish. Still the "penny supper" lives on. Today it is called *cena familia* (family supper) and the dishes, usually Mexican and Central American specialties, are a good deal spicier than years ago. But the food is still made from scratch, and the community spirit is as strong as ever.

Things may have changed, but things are still good, very good, indeed, for those who crave the local flavor and fellowship of a community gathering, those who prefer living traditions to trendy restaurants, and those who appreciate a little meaning with their meal. ❧

(A version of this essay appeared in the January/February 1997 issue of *Wisconsin Trails*.)

Of Hogs and Men: The Folks Who Build and Ride the Legendary Harley

by Tom Walker

"There may be some confusion as to what the Harley-Davidson Motor Company actually is. Some call it an American icon. Others call it a business success story. Starched shirts call it a good investment. Well, we're not sure about any of that, but we do know one thing: we build motorcycles. And we build them pretty gosh darn good."—www.Harley-Davidson.com

There really is nothing like a Harley. In name, logo, and legend, the Harley-Davidson motorcycle enjoys a mystique of legendary proportions. The Harley legend has even mixed company with Elvis and James Dean in the recent circulation of an "urban legend" involving one of the several blue Harleys Elvis owned.

But the Harley mystique is best embodied in the motorcycle itself.

You hear it in the quintessential rumble of the V-Twin engine's firing pattern—two firings in quick succession followed by a long, dead space as the large, heavy flywheel makes its round.

You see it in the factory styling of a production bike that riders then customize by adding accessories or "changing the sheet metal," such as gas tanks and other parts.

You feel it in its sheer mass, the low center of gravity, the low-end torque and power.

Some would even say Harleys have souls.

When you're astride one, they'll tell you, you'll know for sure. Harleys not only pervade the senses but may even metaphysically extend them.

Most Harley owners are male (91 percent, down from 98 percent ten years ago),

and riders constitute a fraternity. Strangers will stop on the road to admire each other's bikes. Factory styling and personalized customization ensure that few bikes will be exactly the same. Even non-owners enter into the mystique by wearing a T-shirt or tattoo bearing the familiar Harley-Davidson bar and shield.

Harleys have taken on an almost totemic significance. The American-made, heavyweight Harley stands for individualism, pluralism, and liberty, evoking the spirit of freedom on the open road. The association of Harleys with the Hell's Angels and other motorcycle gangs during the 1960s probably pushed these centrist values to an anarchist extreme. The company may have wanted to dissociate itself from the image of the free-wheeling outlaw biker, but outlaws preferred Harleys because of their weight and power and also because they could be easily stripped, chopped, or otherwise customized. Whether or not Harley riders promote political values—anarchist, libertarian, or otherwise—traces of the associations of rugged individualism persist in the romance with black leather, blue jeans, and highly stylized hogs.

The nickname "hog" for Harley has also become an acronym for the company-sponsored Harley Owners Group. Now some 300,000 strong, HOG embodies the company's commitment to building rapport with its "family" of riders. HOG organizes rides and rallies for this widely dispersed community and serves as a clearinghouse for information. Activities include small, impromptu early morning rides, large regional rallies, and the "coming home" event in June 1998 for the 95th Anniversary. Motoring together is a display of solidarity

"When you're astride one, they'll tell you, you'll know for sure. Harleys not only pervade the senses but may even metaphysically extend them."

These outfits are typical of what the Harley-Davidson clothing line offered in the 1940s and 1950s and representative of what members of motorcycle clubs wore during that era. This couple is posing on the Harley-Davidson 1949 Duo-Glide.

and often a way to find out who and how many really belong.

The Harley logo has taken on a mystique of its own. Harley-Davidson's merchandising of clothing and accessories is a carefully cultivated aspect of the company's business success. Harley employees model the successful line of rider clothing for the catalog, and one of the union officers creates an ideal image of the Harley rider—tall, physically fit, with long silver hair and mustache.

The four founders of the Harley-Davidson Motor Company posed for this photograph outside their headquarters in early 1912. From left to right: Arthur Davidson, Walter Davidson, William S. Harley, and William Davidson.

production base of the FL line.

The company produces plastics and fiberglass at a third facility, in Tomahawk, Wisconsin, while the chassis and final assembly plant is located in York, Pennsylvania. The plant moved to Pennsylvania while the AMF Corporation owned Harley-Davidson in the 1970s. One of the company's proudest moments involves raising the capital to buy the company back from AMF in 1981. Many measure the company's turnaround in quality standards from this period.

Production workers make decisions about setting or changing production levels or assessing quality and safety standards within their work groups. "Work group advisors" have replaced supervisors, and union representatives participate regularly in leadership meetings. One of them serves as employee involvement coordinator.

Harley workers take great pride in their work. Many are also Harley riders and owners who periodically trade up or upgrade their bikes.

Harley-Davidson maintains other divisions that support the production process, including a tool and die shop and a machine repair shop. The tool and die shop employs the engineers who design and make prototypes for many of the tools used in the production process. At the machine repair shop, skilled tradesmen repair tools and line production equipment.

One craftsman in this shop, Dan Ehlers (otherwise known as "Yooper"), has invented several hand tools to aid him in his work, great stuff like special short handled screw-

The mystique that surrounds the rider also pervades the corporate and shop floor cultures at Juneau Avenue and Capitol Drive in Milwaukee, where official names for some of the older engines, the "blockhead," the "knucklehead," the "pan head," were adopted from the vernacular of the riders.

In business lingo, Harley-Davidson is a "learning company." It has achieved excellent labor relations, developed a family presence in ownership and management, reorganized work relations based on employee involvement, and responded to and incorporated the moods and tastes of the rider culture.

And they're growing at a phenomenal rate. The company plans to double its production rate within five years. The Capitol Drive plant in Wauwatosa, Wisconsin, is expanding production of the XL or sportster engine and transmission to fill the space left by the migration of the FL engine and transmission to the new Pilgrim Road plant (formerly a Briggs and Stratton plant) in Menomonee Falls. The Pilgrim Road plant will also house an expanded

drivers for tight places, wheel pulling devices for hard-to-grip flywheels, adjustable pinch bars—all beautifully crafted, mostly on a metal lathe, and developed from his years of experience at Harley and elsewhere.

Another Harley craftsman, Roy Treder, a retired millwright and welder from the plant maintenance department, creates sculptures out of scrap engine parts such as connecting rods, valves, pistons, spark plugs, rocker covers, whatever. Treder has made more than 200 sculptures for retirees in his thirty-seven years with the company. Each sculpture bears the trademark Harley-Davidson bar and shield, and most are functional as clocks or desk lamps or the like. Treder fashions each creation with parts from the department where the employee worked. For a retired janitor, he actually fashioned a scale model dumpster as part of the sculpture.

As with Treder's career mini-monuments, a personalized bike represents its owner and the workers who built it. In the words of Willie G. Davidson, the company's premier designer, each Harley is a "rolling sculpture." His words pay

The first Harley-Davidson factory was this ten- by fourteen-foot structure built with supplies contributed by the father of the Davidson brothers. The first prototypes and the first motorcycles were built here on the Davidson family lot on what is now the corner of Highland and 37th in Milwaukee. From these modest beginnings Harley-Davidson, now in its 95th year, has risen to become a major corporation employing an estimated 6,000 people.

tribute to the roughly 6,000 people who make the Harley-Davidson—the bike and the myth. ❧

JACK TANKKA
RETIRED FROM
HARLEY-DAVIDSON
11/30/64 - 12/31/96

Harley-Davidson craftsman Roy Treder creates commemorative sculptures, clocks, and other items from scrap engine parts as keepsakes for retiring employees. Each piece bears the company's trademark bar and shield.

The Harmony Bar Upholds Wisconsin Tavern Tradition

by Gina Grumke

> *"When I left Wisconsin in my twenties, I was surprised to realize that most of the country didn't share this idea of the tavern as a comfortable gathering place for all family members."*

When I was a child, a perfect meal consisted of a greasy hamburger topped with a slice of raw onion, accompanied by crinkle cut french fries slathered with Heinz ketchup, served in a waxed paper-lined plastic basket, and washed down with an ice cold, syrupy Coke. My brothers and I also enjoyed beer nuts, sour cream and onion potato chips, maraschino cherries, and Slim Jims. We were not quite adventurous enough to try the pickled eggs but did relish "Blind Robins," a salty dried herring snack, and "Weasel Peters," a dried beef stick.

Meals this wonderful were only served in the neighborhood tavern—a dark, heavenly place that smelled of fried food and cigarette smoke and offered mysterious diversions that flickered, beeped, and squawked. We were endlessly fascinated with a moving Hamm's beer sign that continually revisited an inviting riverside campsite with a realistic campfire somewhere in the North Woods. We pestered our parents endlessly for quarters to fill the pinball machines, jukeboxes, and pool tables.

The adults here, including our parents, talked and laughed more than they did at home and tolerated our kid behavior and exuberance.

Local taverns have been community gathering places in Wisconsin since European settlement. For as long as I can remember, people have described tiny settlements as "just a post office and a couple of bars." The social fabric of Wisconsin has undergone tremendous changes since the days of "a bar on every corner." We're more health conscious now, we heed stiffer drunk driving laws, and our entertainment choices are no longer limited by how far we can walk. Yet taverns and bars continue to thrive and to provide a cornerstone of social life.

When I left Wisconsin in my twenties, I was surprised to realize that most of the country didn't share this idea of the tavern as a comfortable gathering place for all family members. Instead they were viewed as places to imbibe liquor, consort with unsavory characters, and generally get yourself in trouble. I was puzzled by what I encountered in other regions of the country: bars closed on Sundays, private "clubs" to circumvent restrictive liquor laws, "dry" towns, state run liquor stores with lab-coated sales staff.

In the 1980s I spent a summer working in Germany and discovered the neighborhood *Stuben*. All the elements of Wisconsin taverns were there: a limited menu of soup and sandwiches, beer on tap, a jukebox, a couple of electronic games, and a local (within walking distance) crowd. The Wisconsin taverns that I grew up around are close cousins of these neighborhood *Stuben*.

Tavern owners are usually small businesspeople who work a shift behind the bar serving drinks, making burgers, and keeping order. Bars are housed in long, narrow buildings, filled with a counter, bar stools, a couple of tables, a pool table, and some pinball machines. Most bars have at least a small grill and fryer, and some have full kitchens in back. Many bars have an attached "dining room" for eating, a performance space for bands, and room for parties and other special celebrations.

Madison's Harmony Bar sits on the corner of a busy crosstown artery and a residential street, where a couple of connected two story storefronts have housed a bar since at least the 1930s. Signs out front proclaim "Bar" and "Grill," and a

Neighborhood taverns such as the Harmony Bar in Madison have long been community gathering places and are definitely part of the social fabric of Wisconsin.

couple of neon beer signs light the small windows.

Regulars enter by the side door; only new customers use the front door. Bartenders and customers greet each other by name and inquire about each others' lives. "Did you catch the softball game last night?" "Where's your wife working now?"

During the day people drift in and out, drink coffee, read the paper, watch news or sports on the televisions, and chat with the bartenders, many of whom have worked there for years. A constant stream of delivery people bring beer, hard liquor, and food. Around 11:30 a.m. the lunch rush starts—workers from the area, government office staff who have driven from the Capitol Square, and folks from the neighborhood.

After lunch people start coming in for a beer or two, maybe a bowl of soup, a plate of stuffed jalapeño peppers or a basket of homemade chips and dip. There are decks of cards and cribbage boards behind the bar for the asking. The telephone rings frequently. Many calls are for customers the bartenders know, so they rarely have to yell out someone's name.

In the adjoining dining room, with its black and white checked tile floor and beautiful tin ceiling, customers rearrange the tables and chairs to accommodate groups eating, drinking, and playing cards. The tables hold infant carriers, birthday cakes, and presents. Folks bring their own party decorations, including embarrassing photo montages of the guest of honor or signs of farewell, good luck, or congratulations.

The dining room also houses electronic dart machines, Boston Celtics basketball team posters, framed posters, and announcements of past concerts or dances at bar. When there's no band playing, the stage becomes more dining space. Elaborate menu boards, part poster, part movable letter and chalk boards, announce the regular menu and the specials. A changing display of kitsch includes tropical masks and baseball hats and T-shirts. A back bar sports mirrors and glass-doored cabinets filled with liquor bottles.

On a typical summer evening, the bar and dining room are packed with softball teams. Players relax with burgers, brats, homemade pizza, or the one of the nightly specials, washed down with pitchers of one

A Celebration of Wisconsin Traditions • **55**

Tavern amusements such as cards, dice, darts, and pool are popular and relaxing pastimes for many Wisconsinites. Folks also get together at the Harmony for company and to enjoy live music or sporting events on television.

This player might seem "poker-faced" but the name of the card game at the Harmony Bar is unmistakably sheepshead.

of the many regional beers on tap. Kids run around or play darts and pinball. The jukebox booms out Stevie Ray Vaughan, B.B. King, or the Rolling Stones. A friendly pool game dominates the back of the barroom, and a line of quarters indicates challenges to "ownership" of the table.

An avid sheepshead player, co-owner Keith Daniels instigates a daily card game in the front of the bar. The several large televisions mounted high on the walls mime sporting events, except during playoffs and anything involving the Packers, when the play-by-play blares full blast. On weekends live music dominates the dining room.

The management displays a '90s ambivalence toward smoking. Folks can light up, but there's no cigarette machine. A few brands are available behind the bar at very high prices. Daniels and his wife, Jo Raggozino, opened the bar in 1990. Keith was born and raised outside of Milwaukee, in Burlington, Wisconsin, and spent his youth helping out in the family bar, also called the Harmony Bar. He left Wisconsin for a while but returned with Jo and a strong sense of what kind of bar he wanted to open. When he, Jo, and a partner bought the bar, it was, Keith admits, "a dump," with no customer base to build on. Keith designed the Harmony to be a place where he'd like to hang out with his friends, packing the jukebox with his favorite blues,

"Regulars enter by the side door; only new customers use the front door. Bartenders and customers greet each other by name and inquire about each others' lives."

rock, and jazz, stocking local and regional beer, and building a menu of tasty bar food. He created a corps of regulars in their thirties, making sure that women could come to the Harmony without being hassled. Although the clientele is primarily from the neighborhood, people drive there from all over the city.

Jo was raised on the east coast and was not familiar with the Wisconsin neighborhood tavern, but she has embraced the concept wholeheartedly. She takes care of the food at the Harmony, offering wonderful examples of traditional Wisconsin bar food hamburgers, cheeseburgers, french fries, deep-fried onion rings, fried mushrooms, and cheese curds. Using her skill and vision, and fresh vegetables from her father-in-law's garden, Jo has expanded the menu with specials such as quesadillas, vegetarian sandwiches, pasta salads, and stir fries. She recently installed a pizza oven and serves an old-fashioned thin crust pizza, complete with gobs of cheese and toppings.

The Harmony sponsors darts, basketball, pool, and volleyball teams, but the undisputed favorite is softball. The Harmony Bar sponsors thirty softball teams, six every night of the season, the largest number of softball teams in Madison. Keith limits the number of teams only because of a lack of space, not a lack of player interest. Teams are expected, but not required, to come in, relax and celebrate after the game. Bartenders keep track of what each team orders on a big chart behind the bar. At the end of the season the team that has spent the most money receives a free pizza and beer party from the bar.

Keith sponsors a daylong all-Harmony softball tournament at the end of the season. He provides the beer, park rental fees, and grills, and everyone brings meat to grill.

The busiest night of the year is a tropical theme party to benefit the Atwood Community Center, and the Harmony sponsors a music stage at the Atwood neighborhood summer festival.

With beer and burgers, card playing, conversation, and celebration, Keith and Jo keep alive the institution of the neighborhood tavern as a vibrant social gathering space. ❦

(A version of this article appeared in *Smithsonian Folklife Festival 1998*.)

A Good Way to Pass the Winter: Sturgeon Spearing in Wisconsin

by Ruth Olson

Photo by Bob Rashid

Sturgeon spearing on Lake Winnebago is a fun family event for Donald Thiel, son Michael, and Rusty the dog. The augur is used for other ice fishing with "tip-ups."

"Until the mid-1800s, lake sturgeon were abundant in the Great Lakes, but commercial fishing almost wiped them out. Not so in Lake Winnebago."

Talk to Bill Casper, and you'll likely get a lesson on the history of that peculiar fish, the sturgeon. Eastern Wisconsin's Lake Winnebago hosts the healthiest population of sturgeon in the world, he'll tell you. Lake Winnebago is eleven miles wide, twenty-eight miles long, and just twenty-two feet deep at its deepest point. "It was shoved in here by the glacier," Bill says. "You can tell by all the north and south running lakes in the Great Lakes area. Even Lake Michigan got sort of plowed in here by the great glacier pushing its way down here, and all of these lakes run north and south. Must have been quite a time," he concludes.

Bill believes the sturgeon came into the Great Lakes and Winnebago area from the runoff of the glacier, following rivers like the Mississippi north. Sturgeon have been around for three or four million years.

They are a primitive fish, decades old and yards long. Bill describes them as "a very nice fish to eat." Instead of bones, they have a marrow, a soft, cartilage-like bone. They have gizzards, like dinosaurs and chickens. Covered with a tough hide, sturgeons' backs and sides are ornamented with "scoots" or hackles. Their heads are a heavy mass of bone.

Until the mid-1800s, lake sturgeon were abundant in the Great Lakes, but commercial fishing almost wiped them out. Not so in Lake Winnebago. The lumber boom in the area resulted in a number of dams on the Fox River between the lake and Green Bay, trapping the sturgeon in Lake Winnebago. The Wolf River still runs 125 unrestricted miles before reaching the Shawano dam, giving the sturgeon ample place to spawn and making them self-sustaining.

Spearing sturgeon on the lake has long been a tradition. Bill remembers going out with his Uncle Ambrose, who came up from Milwaukee on weekends to fish. "I'd always want to go with him," Bill says. "And so my mom said, 'Well, you've gotta be eight years old at least.' So when I was eight and he showed up, I started going with him."

They'd leave when it was almost dark and drive out on the lake. "We had to shovel our way out there because there were no snowplows at that time," he says. They'd fish "till we couldn't see any more down in the hole" and then come up to supper.

"I would see him spear sturgeon like you wouldn't believe," Bill recalls.

"And it was at a time where you could get five fish. Well, some days we'd get two." In those years there weren't very many fishermen. "There was a group of us, we fished at Pipe, you know, maybe two miles out," Bill says. "And there was a little group would go to Calumetville and Brothertown. And Quinney. And Stockbridge had a group of fishermen. But south of Pipe and toward Fond du Lac there were hardly ever any shanties at all."

It's different today. Bill estimates that during sturgeon spearing season, the second Saturday through the third weekend in February, there can be three to four thousand shanties on the lake and of course that same number of pick-up trucks. On opening day, thousands of people go out there.

Twenty-four hours before the season starts, people can cut their holes in the ice, producing a block of ice about four feet by six feet and two-and-a-half feet thick. Cutting through that ice requires a chain saw with a special ice bar forty-two inches long. They cut ice at an angle—narrow on top, wider on the bottom—to make it easier to push the ice block into the water. They use long pike poles to sink the block under the ice.

Then they drag the ice shanty over the hole. A shanty typically has two doors in the floor that raise to expose only the four-by six-foot rectangle of water. The sturgeon spearer can sit on a nice dry carpeted floor, in a heated shanty, while waiting to spot a fish.

Photos by Bob Rashid

ABOVE: "Butch" Thiel of Sheboygan settles into his shanty, hoping his decoy will attract a sturgeon.

BELOW: Sturgeon are brought to one of the Wisconsin Department of Natural Resources weigh-in stations where the fish is measured and weighed and its gender recorded. This information is useful to the DNR efforts to track the sturgeon population.

Photo by Bob Rashid

Stacy Blanck of New Holstein proudly displays her catch.

In the old days, when Bill fished with his Uncle Ambrose, they sawed the hole by hand with ice saws, and once they had a hole cut, they didn't move. Now, with a chain saw, a shanty can be set up in twenty minutes. Like most spearers today, Bill just hires someone with a chain saw to cut his hole. "A big chain saw is so very expensive," he notes, "so a guy will buy a big saw, and he'll go out there and cut holes for ten bucks apiece. People will leave their name at a tavern, or he's got a radio in his truck with a flasher on the roof, and you can usually spot him out there, and you just go over and say, 'Hey, I'm over here. When you're ready, come cut a hole for me.' It works out very nicely. He has all the gear for sinking the block, he'll help you move your shanty on the hole, and then he'll leave and cut the next hole."

People may move three times a day. "Some guys spend more time cutting holes than they do fishing," Bill says, but he stays put.

Sturgeon fishing requires a lot of waiting. Some people wait for two or three years to see a fish. Some, in half an hour, see a fish or maybe two. Bill's had pretty good luck over the years getting his sturgeon. He tries to get closest to the spot where he caught a fish the year before, which can be tough, he admits, because, "you can't mark the ice."

Or he might turn on the radio he keeps in the shanty to listen to Jerry Schneider's hourly sturgeon report on the Chilton radio station. "If you get a sturgeon in the morning and you take it in and register, it'll automatically get called in to Jerry Schneider's radio station," Bill explains. "So everybody on the lake will know who got it—there's no secrets any more."

As soon as they hear the news, they start moving. "If they know where I'm at," Bill reports, "and they know someone else near me and if we happen to both get a fish, they'll say, 'Wow, they're in there.' Shanties will come in, move in, and they'll be cutting holes around you, chain saws are going."

Some mornings Bill arrives at his shanty to find perhaps four shanties out with him. But by evening, "you could be right in the middle of a big town," he says. "Like, I'm telling you, they move that fast."

Sturgeon For Tomorrow

Bill Casper founded Sturgeon For Tomorrow (SFT) in 1977, after he decided there was a need to learn how to raise sturgeon artificially in case something happened to the healthy fish population. He printed up bulletins, posted them in local taverns, and had 150 fishermen show up at his meeting.

With the help of William Ballard of Dartmouth College, who had studied sturgeon in Russia and Rumania, SFT spearheaded the effort to hatch sturgeon artificially.

Today, the Wisconsin Department of Natural Resources manages to hatch more than 90 percent of the fertilized eggs. They have helped to restock sturgeon in the surrounding states and even Canada. SFT continues to work closely with the DNR, as members serve on a sturgeon advisory board and help staff a volunteer patrol every spring to stop poaching on rivers while vulnerable fish are spawning.

When SFT started, 11,500 sturgeon inhabited Lake Winnebago; now, estimates put the population at 45,000 to 50,000 fish.

But life on the ice is more sociable than competitive. People stop to visit each other's shanties, maybe sharing a beer while they sit and talk. Many people have CB radios in their shanties and chat back and forth. Like most shanties, Bill's is equipped not only with a heater but with a two burner gas plate. "If you spend a whole day out there, you have to do a little cooking," he says. "If somebody visits, you gotta have a bowl of chili."

Many gather in the taverns in the evening. "Years ago, a guy would walk in with a sturgeon on his shoulder and flop it on the tavern floor, even on the bar," Bill recalls. "Now, of course, they don't want you to do those things. It's always kind of a fun time, you know. And it's a good way to pass the winter in Wisconsin."

Bill's sister Mary Lou Schneider not only spears sturgeon, she carves the decoys she uses to attract them. She's gained local popularity as a decoy maker. Decoys are one of the most important elements in sturgeon spearing, Bill says, and everyone has a favorite. They can range from brightly painted carved wooden fish weighted down with lead, to corn cobs, to kettles. "I've seen washing machine agitators down in the sturgeon holes," Bill says. "People do use weird things out there. They solder cans together

"Sturgeon fishing requires a lot of waiting. Some people wait for two or three years to see a fish. Some, in half an hour, see a fish or maybe two."

and paint it colors. There's a lot of different things out there, piece of stovepipe, who knows? Whatever got lucky a year ago or two years ago, that's what they like to use."

Many people use spears with detachable heads. Once the fish is speared, the handle comes free, exposing the rope attached to the spear head. But Bill prefers the traditional gaff. "When you first hit the fish," he explains, "it will just stop. And if you bring it up right away, and you've got a gaff hook, depending on how you got him, you can take him right outside before he gets too wild on you."

If instead you leave the fish alone for a while and it revives, "they'll take off like a wild calf on a rope," Bill says. "And they're all over the place, down in the mud and up against the ice, and down and up. You will not believe. And then when they come up into the shanty with you, there's water flying, water on the stove. The tail is going! If you get a big fish, eighty pounds, every swat of the tail, seems like five gallons of water comes up at you."

Even so, one person can usually bring the fish out of the lake. Mary Lou speared one that was two pounds heavier than she was, Bill insists. She weighed 115 pounds, and the fish was 117 pounds. She got it out by herself.

It's not just the fish or the company that keep people sturgeon spearing. For many being on the ice is a statement of who they are—as displayed by their personal ice shanties. After Bill bought a couple of rafters from a World War II Quonset hut and built his shanty, his wife, Kathy, suggested that it looked like a big helmet. So he painted it to look like a Green Bay Packer helmet. Bill built his shanty in 1967—the first year the Packers went to the Super Bowl. "Then I went through some tough years with the Packers, you know."

Bill's shanty is easy to find. "If you have your radio, they'll say, 'He got one in the Packer helmet!'" Bill reports. He doesn't mind that people like to come and visit. "You just sit and talk and fish," he says. 🐟

Photo by Bob Rashid

Trip's Tapsidermy, a tavern in Pipe, Wisconsin, shows the local fascination with sturgeon spearing.

(A version of this article appeared in *Smithsonian Folklife Festival 1998*.)

Contributors

Wisconsin native **Terese Allen** went from restaurant management to writing when she authored *The Ovens of Brittany Cookbook*. Her *Fresh Market Wisconsin* celebrates the glories of the state's farmers' markets and roadside stands and her third book, *Wisconsin Food Festivals*, combines cookbook and guide to crop and heritage festivals. Allen is contributing editor and food columnist for *Wisconsin Trails*.

Michael J. Chiarappa earned a Ph.D. from Pennsylvania and is currently assistant professor in the department of history at Western Michigan University in Kalamazoo. He focuses on maritime, community, and public history, folklife, and historic preservation. He also directs the Great Lakes Center for Maritime Studies, a collaborative research and educational venture involving the university and the Michigan Maritime Museum.

Gina Grumke, a Wisconsin native, has done fieldwork relating to Wisconsin taverns and is now completing her dissertation at the University of Wisconsin–Madison. She is currently employed by the Doblin Group, a Chicago-based innovation planning firm.

Richard March holds a Ph.D. in folklore from Indiana University and has been the folk arts specialist for the Wisconsin Arts Board since 1983. Since 1986 he has been the producer and on-air host of *Down Home Dairyland*, a program featuring the traditional and ethnic music of the Midwest on Wisconsin Public Radio. He is active as a polka musician, playing button accordion in the Down Home Dairyland Band.

Ruth Olson is a folklorist who has taught at Harvard University, the University of Pennsylvania, and the University of Wisconsin–Madison. She has done extensive fieldwork on the occupational, recreational, and ethnic life of rural communities in Wisconsin, and is on the staff of the Wisconsin Folklife Festival.

Anne Pryor is a cultural anthropologist who specializes in religious traditions and children's folklore. She is also a specialist in folklife education. Currently, she works for the Wisconsin Arts Board on the staff of the Wisconsin Folklife Festival.

Craig Stinson, a native of Wilmington, North Carolina, is currently finishing graduate work in American Studies at George Washington University. His thesis is on the role of food at a Latino Pentecostal church in Virginia. Stinson served as participant coordinator with the 1998 Smithsonian Folklife Festival.

Robert T. Teske is a folklorist who for the last ten years has served as the executive director of the Cedarburg Cultural Center. He is the curator of the traveling exhibition *Wisconsin Folk Art: A Sesquicentennial Celebration*.

Thomas Vennum, Jr., is senior ethnomusicologist for the Center for Folklife Programs and Cultural Studies at the Smithsonian Institution. His books include *Wild Rice and the Ojibway People* and *American Indian Lacrosse*. His recent album, *American Warriors: Songs for Indian Veterans*, won the 1998 Album of the Year at the American Indian Grammies.

Mai Zong Vue is currently working for the State of Wisconsin at the Department of Workforce Development, Bureau of Welfare Initiatives, Office of Refugee Services. She resettled in Wisconsin in 1980 and enjoys teaching and performing Hmong folk songs.

Tom Walker earned his Ph.D. from Indiana University and has worked as an independent contractor in the area of occupational folklife. He is currently coordinator of the Mid-Atlantic Arts Foundation's Delmarva Folklife Project.

Thanks to the Wisconsin Arts Board and the staff of the Wisconsin Folklife Festival for their assistance.

Wisconsin Sesquicentennial Sponsors

Trailblazer

(Contributions of $250,000 or more)
AT&T
S.C. Johnson Wax
The Credit Unions of Wisconsin

Voyageur

(Contributions of $75,000 or more)
Firstar Corporation
Harley-Davidson, Inc.
Marshall & Ilsley Corporation
Milwaukee Journal Sentinel
Outdoor Advertising Association
Philip Morris Companies
    Miller Brewing Company
    Kraft Foods/Oscar Mayer Foods
    Corp.
    Philip Morris USA
Weber-Stephen Products Co.
W.H. Brady Co.
Wisconsin Manufacturers &
    Commerce

Founder

(Contributions of $30,000 or more)
Alliant-Wisconsin Power
    & Light Foundation
ANR Pipeline Company
Blue Cross & Blue Shield United of
    Wisconsin
Color Ink, Inc.
DEC International, Inc.
Fortis Insurance Company
General Casualty Companies
Home Savings
John Deere Horicon Works
Johnson Controls
Kikkoman Foods, Inc.
Kohler Co.
Marcus Theatres Corporation

Michael, Best & Friedrich
Midwest Express Airlines
Nicolet Minerals Company
Northwestern Mutual Life Foundation
Promega Corporation
Robert W. Baird & Co., Inc.
Snap-on Incorporated
Weyerhauser
Wisconsin Central Ltd.
Wisconsin Department of Tourism
Wisconsin Public Service Foundation
Wisconsin State Cranberry Growers
    Association

Badger

(Contributions of $10,000 or more)
3M
Aid Association for Lutherans
Allen-Edmonds Shoe Corp.
Anonymous
A.O. Smith Corporation
Badger Mining Corporation
Briggs & Stratton Corporation
Case Corporation
Consolidated Papers, Inc.
Dairyland Power Cooperative
Eller Media Company
Fort James Corporation
Fraser Papers
Fred Usinger, Inc.
Green Bay Packaging, Inc.
International Paper
Jockey International, Inc.
Jorgensen Conveyors, Inc.
J.P. Cullen & Sons, Inc.
Kimberly-Clark Corporation
Mann Bros., Inc.
Marathon Communications
Marcus Corporation

Marshfield Clinic
Milwaukee Brewers
Modine Manufacturing Company
National Business Furniture, Inc.
Oscar J. Boldt Construction Co.
Pizza Pit, Ltd.
Rockwell Automation/Allen-Bradley
Rust Environment & Infrastructure
Schneider National
Shopko
Stevens Point Brewery
The Edgewater
Twin Disc, Incorporated
United States Cellular
Virchow, Krause & Company, LLP
Walters Buildings
Wausau Mosinee Paper Corporation
    Foundation
Wisconsin Bakers Association, Inc.
Wisconsin Counties Association
Wisconsin Department of Commerce
Wisconsin Physicians Services

Homesteader I

(Contributions of $1,500 or more)
AFSCME
Bill Graham Land & Development
    Co., Inc.
Columbia ParCar of Wisconsin
CUNA Mutual
Discover Wisconsin
Gilbert Paper
Golden Guernsey
Hiebing Group
J.H. Findorff & Son, Inc.
Karen Johnson Productions
Madison Gas and Electric Foundation,
    Inc.
Menasha Corporation

Mills Fleet Farm
Nelson Industries, Inc.
Ocean Spray Cranberries
Rexnord
Safway Steel Products
Sargento Foods, Inc.
Swiss Colony, Inc.
The Finishing Group
Times Printing
Torrance Casting, Inc.
Wausau Insurance Companies
Wisconsin Farm Bureau Federation
Wisconsin Gas, a WICOR Company
Wisconsin Health and Hospital
   Association

Homesteader

(Contributions of $250 or more)
Amcast Automotive
Andes Candies
Apache Stainless Equipment Corp.
Ariens Foundation, Ltd.
Artesyn Technologies
Badger Bearing Co.
Bentley & Sons Construction Services
Berlin Foundry Corporation
Braun Corporation
Broan Mfg., Inc.
Century Fence Co.
Chr. Hansen, Inc.
Contact Rubber Corp.
Cook Composites & Polymers
Cooper Power Systems
Cultural Coalition of Wisconsin
Dan Carter, Inc.
Deltrol Controls
EBI Companies
E.C. Styberg Engineering Co., Inc.
Greater Madison Convention
   & Visitors Bureau
Green Bay Packers
Growmark, Inc.
Hooper Foundation
HUI

Hunt-Wesson, Inc./Swiss Miss
Independent Metals
Jones Dairy Farm
JPC Foundation
Kohl's
LiphaTech, Inc.
Navistar International Transportation
Northern States Power Co.
Oshkosh B'Gosh Foundation, Inc.
Packerland Transport
PLYCO
Pneumatech, Inc.
Rayovac Corporation
R.B. Royal Industries, Inc.
Ripon Foods, Inc.
Rural Mutual Insurance Company
Spacesaver Corporation
Standard Process, Inc.
Strong Funds
Sub-Zero Freezer Co., Inc.
Tele-Communications, Inc. (TCI)
The Masterson Company
The Trane Company
Waukesha County Technical College
Western States Envelope Co.
Wis-Pak, Inc.
WISC-TV Madison
Wisconsin Education Association
   Council
Wisconsin Farm Bureau Federation
Wisconsin Packaging Corporation
Wrought Washer Mfg.

Corporate Contributions

(Contributions of $100 or more)
Amron, L.L.C.
Monroe Truck Equipment, Inc.
Northland Stainless, Inc.

Individual Contributions

Mrs. Frances T. Frazier
James & Linda Heineke
Roger C. Mixter (memory of
   Bette Mixter Holbrook)

Additional In-kind Support

Milwaukee Brewers
Olympus Flag & Banner
Schneider National, Inc.
Usinger
Wisconsin Automobile
   & Truck Dealers Association

Cultural Coalition

State Historical Society of Wisconsin
University of Wisconsin–Extension
Wisconsin Academy of Sciences,
   Arts and Letters
Wisconsin Arts Board
Wisconsin Humanities Council
Wisconsin Public Radio
Wisconsin Public Television

With Cooperation From

AIA Wisconsin
American Automobile Association of
   Wisconsin
Hessen-Wisconsin Society, Inc.
Madison Future Farmers of America
Wisconsin Association of Fairs
Wisconsin Broadcasters Association
Wisconsin Chamber of Commerce
   Executives
Wisconsin Cheese Makers Association
Wisconsin-Chiba, Inc.
Wisconsin Council for Local History
Wisconsin Farm Progress Days, Inc.
Wisconsin Farmers Union
Wisconsin Ginseng Association
Wisconsin Grocers Association
Wisconsin Music Educators
   Association
Wisconsin Newspaper Association
Wisconsin Restaurant Association
Wisconsin Tavern League
Wisconsin Tourism Federation